MOJAVE DESERT
Wildflowers

A FIELD GUIDE TO HIGH DESERT WILDFLOWERS OF
CALIFORNIA, NEVADA, AND ARIZONA

TEXT AND PHOTOGRAPHY BY
JON MARK STEW

D0193342

Text and photography: Jon Mark Stewart

Map: Sue Irwin

Printed and bound in Singapore

Library of Congress Catalog Card Number: 97-62452

ISBN 0-9634909-1-5

Jon Stewart Photography
8020 Dark Mesa Ave NW
Albuquerque, New Mexico 87120

Front cover: California poppy, owl's clover, and goldfields. Antelope Valley.

Title page: Dune primrose, sand verbena, and dune marigold. Johnson Valley.

The Photographs page: Interior goldenbush. Mojave National Preserve.

Back cover: Mojave yucca. Mojave National Preserve.

Regions of the Mojave Desert

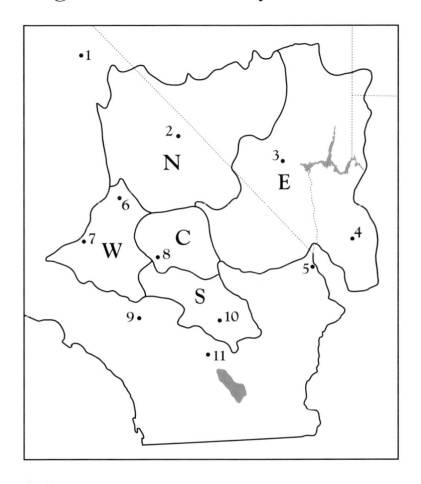

Map of the Mojave Desert showing the major towns and regions.
Bishop (1), Furnace Creek (2), Las Vegas (3), Kingman (4), Needles
(5), China Lake (6), Mojave (7), Barstow (8), San Bernardino (9),
Twentynine Palms (10), Indio (11), southern (S), western (W),
central (C), northern (N), eastern (E).

Preface

Each year there is anticipation of spring in the desert, and each spring thousands of people flock to the deserts with hope that the winter and spring rains have been plentiful. While it is only in rare years that the desert explodes with carpets of flowers, it is well worth the wait. It amazes me that the desert, a place with an exceptionally harsh environment can, under the right conditions, provide one of the most astonishing displays of diversity and color.

It is with pleasure that I offer to the desert wildflower enthusiast this second in a series of wildflower books glorifying the diversity of desert plant life. *Mojave Desert Wildflowers* presents a condensed view of the approximately 1750-2000 species of plants known to occur throughout the Mojave Desert region of southeastern California, northwestern Arizona, southern Nevada, and the extreme southwestern tip of Utah.

My first experiences in the Mojave Desert were as a student at Chaffey College in Alta Loma, California. In spring of 1975, I enrolled in field botany taught by the late Dr. Richard Beeks. We took many field trips during this class, but two were to the Clark Mountains in the east Mojave Desert and to Lucerne Valley in the southern Mojave Desert. These outings created a lasting impression on me. I still remember many of the specimens collected and identified, and nearly all are represented in *Mojave Desert Wildflowers*.

The challenge of assembling a book of this kind is deciding just how much to include. During this project over 170 rolls of film were exposed to capture about 240 plant species plus assorted landscapes. Whittling this down to the 195 species displayed was an arduous task. I had every desire to include them all, regardless of whether they were common or rare, attractive or ugly. My goal, though, was not to produce a wildflower encyclopedia, but rather a usable field guide to the more common, unusual, and interesting wildflowers found in the Mojave Desert.

This guide is designed to be used easily by the wildflower novice, and accurate enough for the seasoned botanist. As in *Colorado Desert Wildflowers*, the chapters are arranged by color, and the plants within the chapters are grouped somewhat taxonomically. This allows plants that are similar in color and appearance to be grouped together, easing identification. Each plant is identified by both its botanical name and common name. In addition, I have included the scientific and common family names and a brief paragraph about each plant. The cacti have been separated into their own chapter at the end of the book because they are a unique group.

The botanical names used here follow the taxonomy of *The Jepson Manual, Higher Plants of California* (Hickman, ed., 1993). For the few plants not contained in *The Jepson Manual*, the scientific name most accepted by the botanical community was used. In the back of the guide is a list that translates the names used in *Mojave Desert Wildflowers* with those that have appeared in older floras such as *A Flora of Southern California* (Munz), and *Arizona Flora* (Kerney and Peebles).

The plants in this book were photographed with the intention of showing as much plant as was reasonably possible. This was done to ensure that enough information was presented in each image so the plant could be identified accurately and with little effort. In some cases, it will be necessary to review the text for size and stature information or for discussion of similar species.

Throughout this guide, scientific terms have been avoided. Where measurements are included in the text, both U.S. and metric dimensions are given since the Mojave Desert receives visitors from every continent.

Books like this can never be done with out the assistance of others. I would like to thank the following individuals for reviewing the text and offering their comments: John Evarts, Esy Fields, Jim Holland, John Hohstadt, Liz Mason, Mike McGill, Tim Rash, Alan Romspert, and Andy Sanders.

The following very special people deserve a warm thanks for reviewing the text, offering their encouragement, and being the best of friends: Cam & Katie Barrows, Mark & Tracy Fisher, Al & Terrie Muth, and John & Jen Purcell. May we again camp among Joshua trees!

Last person to thank is my wife, Nylia, who offered unending support, accompanied me on the many trips into the Mojave Desert to explore for wildflowers, assisted when the wind blew, read the maps as I drove, and who, on occasion, found plants I didn't see.

Jon Mark Stewart
Albuquerque, New Mexico
November, 1997

Contents

White
Flowers

Dune Evening Primrose Display
Johnson Valley

DESERT LILY, AJO LILY
Hesperocallis undulata

Lily Family
Liliaceae

Desert lily is a surprising plant to find in the desert. It blooms in the Mojave Desert mostly between March and May with fragrant flowers that resemble the cultivated Easter lily. The plant grows about 18 inches (45 cm) tall, or much more in favorable years. The leaves and flower spike are produced from a deep underground bulb that was harvested by Native Americans and early Spanish. The bulb has a taste like garlic, hence its other common name, ajo lily, from a Spanish word that means garlic.

SINGLE-LEAVED ONION
Allium nevadense

Lily Family
Liliaceae

Single-leaved onion is an uncommon plant in the Mojave Desert and a very desirable find. The plant is small with a short stem 2-6 inches (5-15 cm) tall. Only one or two leaves are produced and notice that the leaves are tightly coiled at the tip. The flowers are white to pink, with a darker mid-vein. It is found in sandy soils of the east Mojave and Nevada.

BANANA YUCCA
Yucca baccata

Lily Family
Liliaceae

Banana yucca, also known as blue yucca, closely resembles the Mojave yucca, but its leaves have a bluish cast, and the flowers of banana yucca are longer, between 2 and 5 inches (5-13 cm) long. In addition, while banana yucca can have a small trunk, mature Mojave yuccas are very distinctly trunked. The flowers and fruit were eaten by Native Americans who also used leaf fibers to manufacture sandals, baskets, and rope. It is found mostly on dry slopes in the mountains of the east Mojave between 3000 and 5000 feet (900-1500 m) elevation.

MOJAVE YUCCA
Yucca schidigera

Mojave yucca is commonly found throughout the Mojave Desert on dry rocky slopes and sandy plains below 5000 feet (1500 m) elevation. The flowers are less than 2 inches (5 cm) long. The plant usually produces a trunk between 3 and 6 feet (1-2 m) tall, but one individual in the east Mojave is over 20 feet (6 m) tall. Native Americans used the leaf fibers for rope, sandals, and baskets. The fruits were eaten raw, roasted, or ground into meal. The stringy fibers along the leaf margins are a characteristic shared with the banana yucca.

JOSHUA TREE
Yucca brevifolia

Lily Family
Liliaceae

Joshua tree is a Mojave Desert indicator species found on gentle bajadas across the entire Mojave Desert. Dense forests can be found near Cima in the east Mojave, and near Dolon Springs, Arizona. Starting in March and continuing into May, the waxy, creamy-white flowers are produced in tight clusters on the branch tips. The flowers can be overwhelmingly fragrant around dawn and dusk. Early Mormon settlers gave this plant its common name because it reminded them of the prophet Joshua with his arms raised to the heavens.

GIANT NOLINA
Nolina parryi

Lily Family
Liliaceae

Giant nolina is found mostly on dry slopes of the Little San Bernardino and Eagle Mountains around Joshua Tree National Park and in the northern Mojave's Kingston Mountains. Some plants can have trunks 2 feet (60 cm) in diameter and be over 12 feet (4 m) tall when in bloom. The white, plume-like flower stalk appears in May or June. There are separate male and female plants, and only female plants will remain plume-like in the summer and fall when loaded with seed.

YERBA MANSA
Anemopsis californica

Lizard's-Tail Family
Saururaceae

Yerba mansa, meaning "gentle herb," is common in wet, sub-alkaline places in all regions of the Mojave Desert. The plant spreads from a creeping rootstock and forms patches along springs and seeps. In spring and summer the flowers are produced in a spike subtended by 5-8 white, petal-like bracts. This plant had extensive medicinal uses by Native Americans. Dried roots and stems were used to heal sores, and a tea from the roots was used to cure stomach ulcers.

MOJAVE PRICKLY POPPY

Argemone corymbosa

Poppy Family
Papaveraceae

This fragrant flowered poppy is common in the eastern Mojave Desert especially around Cima and Kelso. It is displaced by desert prickly poppy (*A. munita*) in lower elevation areas such as Death Valley, Lake Mead, and Joshua Tree National Park. Mojave prickly poppy is very similar to desert prickly poppy but has orange sap instead of yellow, less than 120 stamens in the flower (vs. >150), and the leaves are generally less prickly on the upper surface as the lower. It grows on dry slopes and in sandy, generally disturbed places such as washes and roadsides.

MOJAVE SAND VERBENA
Abronia pogonantha

Four-O'Clock Family
Nyctaginaceae

Mojave sand verbena is similar to the magenta-flowered hairy sand verbena (p. 130) but usually occurs at higher elevations and has white or pink flowers. It is found in sandy soils mostly in the western Mojave, but ranges through the Mojave Desert to western Nevada. It grows at elevations between 2000-5000 feet (600-1500 m).

WISHBONE BUSH
Mirabilis bigelovii

Four-O'Clock Family
Nyctaginaceae

This common plant is a low, rounded shrub usually found in rocky soils, especially along washes and in canyons. The flowers are funnel shaped and $^1/_4$-$^1/_2$ inch (8-12 mm) long. They appear in spring and early summer and are usually open only in the morning and evening, or on cloudy days. The common name alludes to the wishbone type of stem branching.

CALIFORNIA BUCKWHEAT

Eriogonum fasciculatum

Buckwheat Family

Polygonaceae

California buckwheat is a common shrub found in desert scrub communities, in washes, or on dry slopes and plains. The flowers are white or pinkish and clustered on the end of a long, thin stem. The leaves are about $1/2$ inch (15 mm) long, often with rolled edges. The stems will turn dark red in autumn. It is also known as flat-topped buckwheat.

SPECTACLE-POD
Dithyrea californica

Mustard Family
Brassicaceae

Spectacle-pod is a common spring wildflower found in areas of blowing sand. The white, four-petaled flowers and spectacle-shaped fruits are distinctive. The flowers are also sweetly fragrant. The plant usually grows less than 12 inches (30 cm) tall and is generally multibranched from the base. The leaves are thick, though not fleshy, and covered with hairs.

CLIFF ROSE
Purshia mexicana var. stansburyana

Rose Family
Rosaceae

Like antelope bush, cliff rose is a common shrub with cream-colored flowers. It grows between 3-10 feet (1-3 m) tall on dry slopes and canyons in the mountains of the eastern Mojave. The flowers are exceptionally fragrant with petals $\frac{1}{4}$ inch (6-8 mm) long and produced in profusion. Unlike antelope bush, there are 5-10 fruits per flower that each bear a long, feathery plume about 1-2 inches (3-5 cm) long. The leaves are divided into 3-5 lobes.

MOJAVE ANTELOPE BUSH

Purshia tridentata var. *glandulosa*

Rose Family
Rosaceae

Antelope bush is a widely distributed shrub found in piñon-juniper woodlands. The flowers are cream-colored with petals $1/_4$ inch (6-8 mm) long (shorter than those of apache plume). The flowers produce only one seed and, unlike apache plume and cliff rose, the fruit does not produce a long, feathery plume. The leaves are three-lobed. Antelope bush is an important browse species for both cattle and deer, and grows 3-6 feet (1-2 m) tall or sometimes taller.

APACHE PLUME
Fallugia paradoxa

Rose Family
Rosaceae

Apache plume is one of three similar members of the rose family found in the Mojave Desert. The other two are cliff rose and antelope bush. The flowers of apache plume are white with five petals about $^1/_2$ inch (14 mm) long. After the petals fall, the seeds produce a tuft of long, feathery, reddish plumes that glisten when backlit by the sun. The shrub is about 3-5 feet (1-1.5 m) tall with flaky bark. The leaves are 3-5 lobed with thin segments. Apache plume is common on dry slopes and in sandy washes between 3300-7200 feet (1000-2200 m) elevation.

SILKY DALEA
Dalea mollissima

Silky dalea is a common mat-forming wildflower found on sandy desert plains and in washes below 3000 feet (900 m) elevation. The plant has dark glands along the leaf margins and on the stems. The leaves are hairy and the inflorescence is covered with shaggy hairs. The flowers are white to lavender and shorter than the subtending calyx. East of the town of Twentynine Palms can be found another species, *D. mollis*, which differs by having flower petals longer than the calyx.

DUNE EVENING PRIMROSE
Oenothera deltoides

Evening Primrose Family
Onagraceae

Dune primrose (see p.1) is a common annual on wind-blown sands and is common in the Mojave National Preserve around the Devil's Playground and Kelso Dunes. The exceptionally fragrant flowers are about 1¹/₂-3 inches (4-8 cm) across and open in the early evening. As the plant dries out, the stems curl toward the center and produce a characteristic "bird cage." Dune primrose's nodding flower buds and peeling bark separate this primrose from tufted evening primrose (p. 20), while white evening primrose is a tufted perennial.

WHITE EVENING PRIMROSE
Oenothera californica ssp. *avita*

Evening Primrose Family
Onagraceae

This evening primrose is a tufted perennial found on dry plains mostly in the Joshua tree and piñon-juniper woodland zones. The flowers are about 2 inches (50 mm) wide. The peeling stems and nodding flower buds separate this plant from tufted evening primrose (next page). The leaves are generally less than $2^1/_2$ inches (6 cm) long. A rare subspecies, called the Eureka Dunes evening primrose (*Oe. c.* ssp. *eurekensis*), is found in the northern-most Mojave Desert in the Eureka Valley.

TUFTED EVENING PRIMROSE
Oenothera caespitosa

Evening Primrose Family
Onagraceae

Tufted evening primrose is a low growing plant generally found in rocky or sandy places in the piñon-juniper zone. The flowers are usually 2-3 inches (5-8 cm) across, very fragrant, open in the evening, and fade pinkish the next day. The leaves are narrow with wavy margins and about 1-4 inches (3-10 cm) long. Unlike dune evening primrose and white evening primrose this plant does not have peeling bark, and the flower buds are erect instead of nodding.

SCARLET GAURA
Gaura coccinea

Evening Primrose Family
Onagraceae

Scarlet gaura is an attractive plant found at low- to mid-elevations. In California it is usually associated with Joshua tree woodlands or piñon-juniper woodlands in the mountains of the eastern Mojave. In Arizona and Nevada it can also be quite common in washes around Lake Mead. This perennial shrub is usually less than 20 inches (50 cm) tall, with white flowers that age red.

WOODY BOTTLE-WASHER
Camissonia boothii

Evening Primrose Family
Onagraceae

Woody bottle-washer is common on open plains and washes mostly at lower elevations, but can occur as high as 6000 feet (1800 m). The plant produces a rather compact cluster of flowers at the top, with the leaves located underneath. Unlike brown-eyed primrose, the flowers of woody bottle-washer lack a brown center. Woody bottle-washer acquired its common name from the woody skeleton that remains after the plant dies in late spring or summer. Locally, this plant is also known as desert lantern.

BROWN-EYED PRIMROSE
Camissonia claviformis

Evening Primrose Family
Onagraceae

Brown-eyed primrose is a very common wildflower found in washes and on sandy plains. It is slightly variable with three subspecies described for the Mojave Desert. Characteristic of this flower is the brown center which is not present in the other white flowered evening primroses. The plant is usually about 6 inches (15 cm) tall, but can grow to 18 inches (45 cm) in favorable years. The leaves are mostly clustered at the base of the plant. The fruit is club-shaped and about 1 inch (25 mm) long.

RATTLESNAKE WEED
Chamaesyce albomarginata

Spurge Family
Euphorbiaceae

Rattlesnake weed is an extra low-growing plant found mostly on dry slopes and sandy washes, but can also be found in disturbed areas such as along road cuts. It is very common throughout most of the Mojave Desert. The plant forms a mat between 4-20 inches (10-50 cm) across. The stems and leaves produce a milky sap when broken. What appear to be white petals are really appendages that surround the small flower, which is petal-less and located on a stalk in the center.

SMALL-LEAVED AMSONIA

Amsonia tomentosa

Dogbane Family
Apocynaceae

Amsonia is a shrubby perennial herb about 8-16 inches (20-40 cm) tall with straight stems that bleed a milky sap. Two types of this plant occur in the Mojave Desert — one type with hairy, gray leaves and the other with green leaves. The fragrant flowers are white to bluish or greenish. Amsonia is occasionally found on sandy plains or in washes between 2500-6000 feet (750-1800 m) and can sometimes be locally abundant.

DESERT MILKWEED
Asclepias erosa

Milkweed Family
Asclepiadaceae

Desert milkweed is found mostly in sandy washes and along roadsides below 5000 feet (1500 m) elevation. It is an erect herbaceous perennial that grows over 3 feet (80 cm) tall. The leaves are 3-6 inches (8-15 cm) long and arranged opposite each other on the stems. A large, black wasp, known as the tarantula hawk (*Hemipepsis sp.*), is a frequent visitor to the flowers. When cut, the stems ooze milky sap.

CLIMBING MILKWEED

Sarcostemma cynanchoides ssp. *hartwegii*

Milkweed Family
Asclepiadaceae

Climbing milkweed is one of two species of twining milkweeds found in the Mojave Desert. The other is rambling milkweed (*Sarcostemma hirtellum*), which has densely hairy stems and leaves, and smaller greenish-white flowers. Climbing milkweed is usually found at lower elevations in washes twining over other shrubs and is very common in the southern Mojave and around Lake Mead. The flowers are white with purplish markings. As the common name implies, the stems drip milky sap when cut.

PEACH THORN
Lycium cooperi

Nightshade Family
Solanaceae

Peach thorn is a common plant found mostly below 5000 feet (1500 m) elevation on dry flats and slopes. It is a densely leafy, compact shrub about 3-5 feet (1-1.5 m) tall with thorny branches that go deciduous during the summer. The flowers are greenish-white and bloom March to May. The fruit is a yellow to orange berry with many seeds. Another related shrub found in the Mojave Desert is wolfberry (*L. andersonii*) with spine-tipped branches and light lavender, tubular flowers. Wolfberry is found in washes and on rocky or gravelly slopes.

JIMSON WEED, MOON FLOWER
Datura wrightii

Nightshade Family
Solanaceae

Jimson weed is a common perennial shrub found mostly in open sandy washes and other disturbed places. The plant is quite luxurious for a desert plant growing about 3 feet (1 m) tall. The large funnel-shaped flowers are white, often with a violet tinge, very fragrant, and 6-8 inches (15-20 cm) long. This very toxic, sometimes deadly plant was used by Native Americans as a hallucinogen during religious ceremonies. The flowers are open mostly at night and close during midday.

WHITE GOLDEN GILIA
Linanthus aureus ssp. *decorus*

Phlox Family
Polemoniaceae

This little ephemeral is a white flowered form of golden gilia (p. 81). It is not as common as its yellow relative, and they rarely seem to co-exist. It is found on sandy flats, usually in abundance. The stems are thread-like, and the leaves have 3-7 narrow clefts. The flowers have a maroon throat and open during the day. It is similar to three other *Linanthus* that bloom at night (*L. bigelovii*; *L. dichotomus*, evening snow; *L. jonesii*). These three plants also occur in the Mojave Desert on sandy soils and have white flowers.

PARRY GILIA
Linanthus parryae

Phlox Family
Polemoniaceae

Parry gilia is a common tufted ephemeral found mostly in the western and central Mojave on dry sandy flats. The plant is less than $2^1/_2$ inches (6 cm) tall, and when young, the flowers conceal the plant below. The flowers are mostly white though occasionally blue-purple. Unlike golden gilia, the flowers are not on the end of a thread-like stem. In favorable years the plants can be so dense that the ground appears to be covered with snow.

HUMBLE GILIA
Linanthus demissus

Phlox Family
Polemoniaceae

Humble gilia is a common spring wildflower in washes and on desert pavements. In Death Valley National Park and the Mojave National Preserve it can be exceptionally abundant, but because the plant is small with white flowers, it is frequently overlooked as it blends with the gravel and rock pebbles. The flowers are very fragrant with petals that twist like a windmill. The plant is mostly less than 2 inches (5 cm) tall but can grow to 4 inches (10 cm) in favorable years.

ROUND-LEAF PHACELIA
Phacelia rotundifolia

Waterleaf Family
Hydrophyllaceae

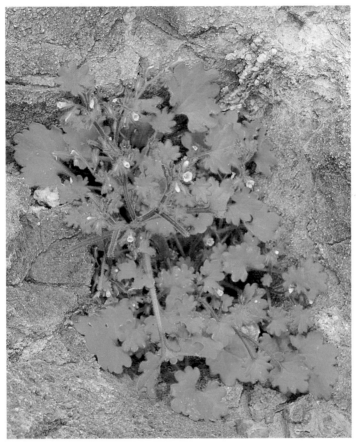

Round-leaf phacelia is a spring annual found in rocky crevices, frequently on limestone, below 6000 feet (2000 m) elevation. The tubular flowers are white, pinkish or pale violet with a yellow tube. The leaves are roundish, mostly $1/_4$-1 inch (5-20 mm) wide, and toothed on the margins. The 2-12 inch (5-30 cm) long stems are slender and very fragile. It is quite common in the limestone mountains of Death Valley National Park and the Mojave National Preserve, extending to Joshua Tree National Park.

WHITE FIESTA FLOWER
Pholistoma membranaceum

Waterleaf Family
Hydrophyllaceae

Fiesta flower is a weak-stemmed ephemeral usually found in the shade of rocks or intertwined with other plants. It grows in the desert at relatively low elevations, mostly below 3500 feet (1000 m). The flowers are about $^3/_8$ inch (1 cm) wide, and as shown, the petals can have purple spots. The stems are brittle and have prickles that are noticeable when the plant is handled.

ALKALI HELIOTROPE
Heliotropium curassavicum

Borage Family
Boraginaceae

Alkali heliotrope is a prostrate to weakly-ascending plant that spreads from a perennial root. The succulent stems are 4-24 inches (10-60 cm) long. It is found in moist to dry alkaline or saline soils such as along the edges of dry lake beds. The leaves and stems are quite fleshy and succulent. The flowers are white to bluish with yellow in the throat that usually turns purple with age. The flowers are borne in a scorpion tail-like spike that uncoils as the flowers open.

SCENTED FORGET-ME-NOT
Cryptantha utahensis

Borage Family
Boraginaceae

Scented forget-me-not is a common spring wildflower found in sandy to gravelly soils below 6500 feet (2000 m) elevation. The small white flowers are scented like carnations. The plant grows erect 4-12 inches (10-30 cm) tall with multiple branches. The seed nutlets are quite distinctive with knife-like or narrowly-winged margins. There are many other species of forget-me-not in the Mojave Desert, and they can be difficult to distinguish.

PIÑON FORGET-ME-NOT
Cryptantha tumulosa

Borage Family
Boraginaceae

Piñon forget-me-not is a simple, erect perennial wildflower found in the higher mountains of the east Mojave and southwest Nevada. It occurs mostly in limestone soils between 4500-6000 feet (1400-1800 m) elevation and is relatively uncommon. The plant grows 3-10 inches (8-25 cm) tall and is covered with either soft or densely stiff hairs. The flowers are white and produced in a loose cylindrical spike.

ARIZONA POPCORN-FLOWER
Plagiobothrys arizonicus

Borage Family
Boraginaceae

This popcorn-flower is an erect to loosely ascending ephemeral that grows about 4-16 inches (10-40 cm) tall. It is very common in the east Mojave below 4000 feet (1200 m) elevation frequently associating with Mojave yucca. The plant starts blooming in March and continues growing and blooming until May or June. The leaves have purple midribs and margins, and the roots have a purple dye. The plant is also known locally as blood-weed because it stains the mouths of cattle red when eaten.

WHITE ASTER
Chaetopappa ericoides

Sunflower Family
Asteraceae

White aster is a low, tufted, erect perennial wildflower found mostly on limestone soils in the mountains of the eastern Mojave. The plant is between 2-6 inches (5-15 cm) tall with many branches arising from a woody base. The leaves are about $\frac{1}{2}$ inch (12 mm) long and covered with stiff hairs. The flowers have a yellow center with white to sometimes pinkish rays.

WHITE WOOLLY DAISY
Eriophyllum lanosum

Sunflower Family
Asteraceae

This woolly daisy is found in sandy soils of the east Mojave eastward into Nevada and Arizona. It is a low growing spring wildflower usually less than 4 inches (12 cm) tall with white-woolly stems. The flowers are about $\frac{1}{2}$ inch (12 mm) wide with white rays and a yellow center. It is frequently found in abundance, though infrequently noticed, because the plant's color blends with the sand and gravel. It is related to the yellow woolly daisy (p. 97) and yellow-frocks (p. 98).

DESERT STAR
Monoptilon bellioides

Sunflower Family
Asteraceae

Desert star is a very common spring wildflower frequently found throughout the eastern, northern, and southern Mojave Desert on sandy and stony plains. The plant grows very low to the ground, and the branches spread 1-3 inches (25-75 mm). It is one of the many desert wildflowers affectionately described as "belly flowers" because admirers must get down on their bellies to enjoy them. The flowers are white with a yellow center and about $1/_2$ inch (15 mm) wide. The flowers close in the evening and reopen the next morning.

WHITE TIDY-TIPS
Layia glandulosa

Sunflower Family
Asteraceae

Look for white tidy-tips in open sandy soils mostly in Joshua tree and piñon-juniper woodlands. The plant is small (6-12 inches; 15-30 cm) and usually few branched. In the eastern and southern deserts the flowers are white with a yellow center. Around Barstow and the Antelope Valley the rays are a creamy white. It is quite common in Joshua Tree National Park, the Mojave National Preserve, and the Antelope Valley.

ROCK DAISY
Perityle emoryi

Sunflower Family
Asteraceae

Rock daisy is a common spring wildflower found on rocky cliffs and dry rocky slopes at mid- to lower-elevations of the Mojave Desert. The plant has bright green foliage that contrasts with the dark desert rocks where it usually grows. The plant has succulent, brittle stems and grows 4-16 inches (10-40 cm) tall. The flowers have white rays with a yellow center.

FREMONT PINCUSHION
Chaenactis fremontii

Sunflower Family
Asteraceae

Fremont pincushion is a common spring wildflower found throughout most of the Mojave Desert below 4000 feet (1200 m) elevation. It usually grows in sandy or gravelly soils such as in washes, or on sandy mesas and alluvial fans. The leaves are green and somewhat fleshy. The plant usually grows between 4-8 inches (10-20 cm) tall. Fremont pincushion is frequently found growing with displays of desert dandelion around Joshua Tree National Park.

MOJAVE PINCUSHION
Chaenactis xantiana

Sunflower Family
Asteraceae

Mojave pincushion is a common spring wildflower found in the western Mojave Desert. It is especially common in the Antelope Valley in sandy soils. The plant grows erect to 16 inches (40 cm) tall with one or more straight branches. A similar plant in the Mojave Desert is Esteve pincushion (*C. stevioides*) with hairy flower stems. It grows mostly on sandy flats and slopes in the southern and eastern Mojave.

WHITE TACK-STEM
Calycoseris wrightii

Sunflower Family
Asteraceae

White tack-stem is a chicory group member related to desert chicory, gravel ghost (next pages) and yellow tack-stem (p. 110). The plant is single- to multi-stemmed with characteristic tack-shaped glands on the stems. White tack-stem grows mostly 4-12 inches (10-30 cm) tall in sandy washes and on gravelly plains and slopes and is only occasionally encountered.

DESERT CHICORY
Rafinesquia neomexicana

Sunflower Family
Asteraceae

Desert chicory is a common spring wildflower usually found in sandy soils below 4500 feet (1400 m) elevation. It is a weak-stemmed plant frequently supporting itself by growing up through other shrubs. The stems can grow as long as 16 inches (40 cm). The flowers are white with rose-purple veins on the outside of each ray flower. Desert chicory is one of several white flowered members of the chicory group found in the Mojave Desert.

GRAVEL GHOST
Atrichoseris platyphylla

Sunflower Family
Asteraceae

Gravel ghost, also known as parachute plant, is fairly common in sandy washes mostly at lower elevations around Lake Mead and Death Valley. Good displays can be found in Death Valley on many of the alluvial fans. The white flowers are about an inch (3 cm) across. The leaves are round-oblong in shape, 1-4 inches (3-10 cm) long, and situated flat on the ground at the base of the tall stems. The leafless stems are mostly 1-3 feet (30-90 cm) tall with inflorescence borne at the tips. In wet years the plants can be taller.

DESERT THISTLE
Cirsium neomexicanum

Sunflower Family
Asteraceae

Desert thistle is a biennial or short-lived perennial found in rocky places of the eastern Mojave to the Lake Mead region. The plant usually forms a prickly rosette of leaves the first year and follows the next spring with a tall, leafy stem topped with flower heads. The plant can be 6 feet (2 m) tall with very spiny leaves. The flowers are white or sometimes pinkish.

Yellow
Flowers

Bear-Paw Poppy
Near Lake Mead

DESERT BARBERRY
Berberis haematocarpa

Barberry Family
Berberidaceae

Desert barberry is an uncommon plant found in piñon-juniper woodlands of the east Mojave around the New York Mountains and nearby McCullough Range. It is a large shrub that grows 3-10 feet (1-3 m) tall with stiff, erect branches and spine-toothed leaves. The flowers are yellow and produce a juicy reddish-brown berry.

BEAR-PAW POPPY
Arctomecon californica

Poppy Family
Papaveraceae

This bear-paw poppy is found on harsh alkaline, gypsum bearing soils in the Lake Mead/Las Vegas region (see p. 50). It is an especially attractive plant about 20 inches (50 cm) tall with large yellow flowers, nodding buds, hairy stems, and three-lobed leaves. It is considered a rare plant due to its limited distribution, though it can be locally quite plentiful. A related plant with white flowers (*A. merriamii*) grows in limestone soils from the Death Valley region to Clark County, Nevada on loose rocky slopes.

CREAM CUPS
Platystemon californicus

Cream cups is a highly variable poppy found on open plains in sandy soils. It is a spring annual that grows less than 12 inches (30 cm) tall. The flowers are cream to yellowish, less than 1 inch (25 mm) across, and solitary on a long, hairy, leafless stem. While found commonly on the coastal side of the mountains, it does reach into the western and central Mojave Desert extending from the Tehachapi Mountains to just south of Barstow. It is especially common in Stoddard Valley, and can form displays along with California poppy in the Antelope Valley.

MOJAVE GOLD POPPY
Eschscholzia glyptosperma

Poppy Family
Papaveraceae

Mojave gold poppy is a common spring wildflower found in washes, on desert plains, and along roadsides throughout most of the Mojave Desert. It is an erect annual with tufted leaves that grows 4-12 inches (10-30 cm) tall. The yellow flowers grow on narrow, leafless stems and nod when in bud. The fruit is a long, narrow capsule $1^1/_2$-$2^3/_4$ inches (4-7 cm) long and contains many little seeds with minute pits.

LITTLE GOLD POPPY
Eschscholzia minutiflora

Poppy Family
Papaveraceae

Little gold poppy is found in washes and on sandy flats and slopes throughout the Mojave Desert. A typical plant has petals less than $^1/_4$ inch (6 mm) long, but plants in the western, northern, and central areas can have longer petals — $^1/_2$-1 inch (10-26 mm) in the western Mojave, and $^1/_4$-$^3/_4$ inch (6-18 mm) in the central and northern Mojave Desert. While the flowers are quite small, the plant is an erect spring wildflower that can grow 14 inches (35 cm) tall.

GOLDEN CARPET
Gilmania luteola

Buckwheat Family
Polygonaceae

Golden carpet is a rare plant restricted to barren alkaline slopes in Death Valley. It is a very localized plant and only grows in exceptionally wet years. The plant is a prostrate spring wildflower with greenish-yellow foliage. The flowers are yellow and very small. While the plant is considered rare, it is certainly worth discovery in years where winter rains have been favorable.

YELLOW PEPPERGRASS
Lepidium flavum

Mustard Family
Brassicaceae

Yellow peppergrass is a common spring ephemeral in the Mojave Desert found in alkaline and sandy soils. It is frequently found on the mud hills around Afton Canyon and Rainbow Basin, though it also occurs in washes and other sandy places. The plant grows prostrate on the ground, and while ususally only about 4-6 inches (10-15 cm) accross the plant can be over 12 inches (30 cm) in favorable years.

PALMER BEAD-POD
Lesquerella tenella

Mustard Family
Brassicaceae

Bead-pod is a spring wildflower found in sandy places at relatively low elevations mostly below 3500 feet (1060 m). The plant has slender ascending stems 4-12 inches (10-30 cm) long without a rosette of leaves at the base and is frequently support by other shrubs. The flowers are yellow to orange and ³/₁₆-¹/₄ inch (5-7 mm) long. The fruit is bead-like and ¹/₈ inch (3-4 mm) wide. In the mountains of the east Mojave is King bead-pod (*L. kingii*), a perennial bead-pod with prostrate to erect stems 2-6 inches (5-15 cm) long and a rosette of leaves at the base.

PRINCE'S PLUME
Stanleya pinnata

Mustard Family
Brassicaceae

Prince's plume is found in washes, on desert slopes, and around dry lake beds throughout much of the Mojave Desert. While it can occur at elevations over 6000 feet (1800 m) it is most commonly found at lower elevations. The plant is 15-60 inches (40-150 cm) tall with deeply lobed leaves and long, dense flower plumes 4-12 inches (10-30 cm) long. The plant will accumulate the toxic mineral selenium from the soil if present. In the Death Valley region is Panamint prince's plume (*S. elata*) that has unlobed leaves.

FALSE CLOVER
Oxystylis lutea

Caper Family
Capparaceae

False clover is another plant restricted to the Death Valley region and nearby Nevada. Unlike other members of the Caper Family found in the desert, this plant has flowers clustered in the leaf axils. The leaves have three elliptic leaflets and the stems are yellowish. The plant is an annual usually growing 1-3 feet (30-90 cm) tall, though in exceptional years it can be taller. Look for this plant on alkali flats and in washes below 2000 ft. (600 m) elevation. It is quite common along the Amargosa River.

MOJAVE STINKWEED
Cleomella obtusifolia

Caper Family
Capparaceae

Mojave stinkweed is a spreading spring wildflower that forms circular mats 3-6 inches (8-15 cm) high and sometimes 3 feet (90 cm) in diameter. The petals are yellow and $1/4$ inch (5-6 mm) long. The leaves are clover-like and covered with fine hairs. The fruits are paired and horn-like at the end of a short ($1/4$ inch, 6 mm long) stem that curves downward. It grows on alkaline flats and slopes.

BLADDER-POD
Isomeris arborea

Caper Family
Capparaceae

Bladder-pod is a common perennial shrub found in desert washes and on sandy plains below 4300 feet (1300 m) elevation. It grows into a rounded shrub 2-5 feet (60-150 cm) tall and has narrow, clover-like leaves. The yellow flowers are about $\frac{1}{2}$ inch (8-14 mm) long. The fruit is an inflated capsule 1-2 inches (25-50 mm) long and $\frac{1}{4}$-$\frac{1}{2}$ inch (5-12 mm) wide. Bladder-pod is related to commercial capers.

COYOTE MELON
Cucurbita palmata

Gourd Family
Cucurbitaceae

Coyote melon is a common perennial vine with stems 1-4 feet (30-120 cm) long that develops from a fleshy, tuber-like root. The plant blooms late spring through summer. The flowers are 2-3 inches (5-8 cm) long and resemble the flowers of cultivated squash and cucumber. The melons are 3-4 inches (8-9 cm) wide and dull green, with greenish-white bands and mottling. Coyote melon grows throughout the Mojave Desert in dry sandy places below 4000 feet (1200 m) elevation. The melons are not edible but were a source of soap for Native Americans.

ROCK NETTLE
Eucnide urens

Stick-Leaf Family
Loasaceae

Rock nettle is a low, rounded bush 1-3 feet (30-100 cm) tall that grows on cliffs, rocky slopes, and in washes below 4000 feet (1200 m). It is especially common in the Death Valley region and around Hoover Dam and Lake Mead. The plant is covered with needle-like, stinging hairs on the leaves and stems and is known locally in Death Valley as sting-bush. The flowers are pale yellow and 1-2 inches (3-5 cm) long.

SAND BLAZING STAR
Mentzelia involucrata

Stick-Leaf Family
Loasaceae

Sand blazing star is a common spring wildflower found on hot desert plains, rocky canyon slopes, and in washes below 3000 feet (900 m) elevation. The plant is 7-14 inches (17-35 cm) tall with irregularly toothed leaves and rough herbage covered with short barbed hairs that give the plant a feeling of sandpaper. The flowers are less than $2^1/_2$ inches (65 mm) long and a cream-yellow color with reddish-orange veins and satiny appearance. In the Mojave Desert it is quite common around Lake Mead.

DUNE BLAZING STAR
Mentzelia multiflora ssp. *longiloba*

Stick-Leaf Family
Loasaceae

Dune blazing star is an erect biennial or perennial 6-40 inches (15-100 cm) tall with few to many branches from the base. It is very common in the Devil's Playground and Kelso Dunes area of the east Mojave Desert. The flowers are golden yellow with ten petals, five of which are really flattened petal-like stamens. Inyo blazing star (M. *oreophila*) is similar to dune blazing star, but differs by having five petals plus an additional five petal-like stamens that are obviously anther tipped. Inyo blazing star grows in washes and on limestone in the desert mountains.

DEATH VALLEY BLAZING STAR
Mentzelia reflexa

Stick-Leaf Family
Loasaceae

Death Valley blazing star is a spring wildflower found commonly in the Death Valley region. It grows in washes and on rocky slopes mostly in Panamint Valley and Death Valley, but sightings have also been made near Kelso in the east Mojave. The plant is rounded, compact, branched at the base, and 1-8 inches (2-20 cm) tall. The eight petaled flowers are $^1/_4$-$^1/_2$ inch (6-12 mm) long and pale yellow.

BLAZING STARS
Mentzelia ssp.

Stick-Leaf Family
Loasaceae

This group of blazing stars are incredibly similar, and telling them apart is quite difficult. About 10 species grow in washes and on gravelly plains throughout the Mojave Desert. The plants are very common annual wildflowers that usually grow less than 16 inches (40 cm) tall. The flowers are yellow and can have an orange spot at the base of each petal. The flowers open in the morning, and vary in size from $^1/_{16}$-1 inch (2-25 mm) long.

HONEY MESQUITE
Prosopis glandulosa var. *torreyana*

Legume Family
Fabaceae

Honey mesquite is common in washes, low depressions, and around springs and seeps. It is the dominant plant on the dunes in Death Valley National Park near Stove Pipe Wells, known as Mesquite Flat Dunes. The plant is a large, many-branched shrub or small tree that has the potential to grow 20 feet (6 m) tall, though usually the plant is significantly shorter. The seed pods are a long bean less than 6 inches (15 cm) long that are favored by wildlife. Mesquite was also a staple of Native Americans who made cakes from the meal.

CATCLAW ACACIA
Acacia greggii

Legume Family
Fabaceae

Catclaw acacia is a common plant found throughout most of the Mojave Desert except at higher elevations above 4600 feet (1400 m). It grows in washes, canyons, and on desert fans. The plant grows as a deciduous shrub or small tree mostly around 6-10 feet (1.8-3 m) tall. Also known as "wait-a-minute" bush, catclaw is abundantly adorned with hooked, claw-like thorns that easily snag clothing. The flowers are composed mostly of yellow stamens and arranged in cylindrical spikes.

HAIRY LOTUS
Lotus strigosus

Legume Family
Fabaceae

Hairy lotus is a common, prostrate spring wildflower found in sandy places below 4500 feet (1400 m). The plant grows low to the ground with stems about 4 inches (10 cm) long. The succulent leaves have 4-9 leaflets and are covered with fine hairs. The flowers are yellow, aging red, on stalks about 0.4 inch (1 cm) long, and are either single or paired in the leaf axils. The fruit is narrow and usually curved at the tip. A similar plant is hill lotus (*L. humistratus*), with broader, elliptic leaves, stalkless flowers in the leaf axils, and a straight, oblong fruit.

DESERT ROCK PEA
Lotus rigidus

Legume Family
Fabaceae

Desert rock pea is a common Mojave Desert perennial found on dry slopes and in washes from Death Valley to the Colorado River. The plant is a somewhat woody shrub that grows 12-36 inches (30-90 cm) tall. The yellow flowers are $^1/_2$-1 inch (12-22 mm) long and turn red or purple with age. During the summer the plant will dry out, go completely deciduous, and look lifeless.

DESERT SENNA
Senna armata

Legume Family
Fabaceae

Desert senna is a common shrub at mid-elevations, especially in Joshua Tree National Park and in the east Mojave. The plant is a rounded shrub about 3 feet (1 m) tall, armed with weak spines, and is leafless most of the year. The flowers are produced profusely in April and May, and the plant is capable of producing broad, colorful displays in sandy washes and open desert plains.

DOUGLAS MILKVETCH
Astragalus douglasii

Legume Family
Fabaceae

Douglas milkvetch is an uncommon perennial milkvetch found in the western Mojave Desert in open grasslands with California poppy. The plant forms mats 16-40 inches (40-100 cm) in diameter. The leaves are 2-6 inches (5-15 cm) long with 11-25 leaflets. The flowers are whitish to pale yellow and about $^1/_2$ inch (8-13 mm) long. The seed pods are very inflated and more than 1 inch (25 mm) long.

MOJAVE SPURGE
Euphorbia incisa

Mojave spurge is found on rocky or sandy slopes from the east Mojave to the Lake Mead region above 3000 feet (1000 m) elevation. The plant is a low perennial 6-16 inches (15-40 cm) high with slender, erect stems that bleed a white, milky sap. What look like yellow petals are actually broad glands with scalloped margins. The flowers are actually petal-less, and the female flowers form a three-lobed fruit on a long stalk.

MOJAVE SUN CUP

Camissonia campestris

Evening Primrose Family
Onagraceae

Mojave sun cup is a common spring wildflower in the western and central Mojave Desert. It grows on open, sandy flats mostly below 3000 feet (900 m). The plant is a slender ephemeral with stems usually less than 10 inches (25 cm) long. The flowers are about 1 inch (25 mm) wide or smaller, with red dots at the base of the petals. The sepals at the base of the petals are attached in pairs. Also in the Mojave, mostly at higher elevations, is tooth-leaved primrose (*C. kernensis*) with four separate sepals.

YELLOW CUPS
Camissonia brevipes

Evening Primrose Family
Onagraceae

Yellow cups is a common spring wildflower found on dry slopes and in washes. The plant flowers when about 2 inches (5 cm) tall and grow to 30 inches (75 cm) later in the season if rains were plentiful. The flowers are yellow with red dots at the base of the petals. While the plant grows up to an elevation of 5000 feet (1500 m), it is more common at lower elevations such as in Death Valley, around Lake Mead, and lower elevations in the east Mojave.

YELLOW EVENING PRIMROSE
Evening Primrose Family
Oenothera primiveris ssp. *bufonis*
Onagraceae

This evening primrose is an occasional spring wildflower found on sandy plains, dune margins, and in washes. The plant is stemless, growing low to the ground, and has hairy leaves $1^1/_2$-5 inches (4-13 cm) long. The yellow flowers open in the evening and turn reddish-orange to purple with age. The petals are 1-$1^1/_2$ inches (25-40 mm) long and have a notch on the end.

CREOSOTE BUSH
Larrea tridentata

Caltrop Family
Zygophyllaceae

Creosote bush is probably the most common shrub in the California Desert. It usually grows 2-6 feet (0.6-2 m) high but can grow taller under ideal conditions. After rains the plant gives off a smell that most people find agreeable and consider a trademark of the southwest desert. The flowers are yellow and can be produced in profusion after wet winters. The flowers are followed by white, fuzzy seed balls that make the plant almost as attractive as when in flower.

THICK-LEAVED GROUND CHERRY

Physalis crassifolia

Nightshade Family

Solanaceae

Ground cherry is a common, low growing shrub found in sandy and rocky places below 4000 feet (1200 m). The plant is intricately branched and 8-20 inches (20-50 cm) tall. The flowers are yellow, about $1/2$ inch (10-15 mm) broad, and resemble the flowers on a tomato, to which ground cherry is related. As the fruit ripens, the leafy base of the flower (sepals) expands to form a lantern over the green berry.

GOLDEN GILIA
Linanthus aureus

Golden gilia is an exceptionally beautiful spring wildflower when it forms brilliant golden patches over large areas in sandy soils. The plant has very slender stems 2-6 inches (5-16 cm) long and funnel-shaped flowers $^1/_4$-$^1/_2$ inch (6-13 mm) long with a darker yellow or maroon throat. A subspecies (*L. a.* ssp. *decorus*, p. 30) with white flowers is occasionally found but not usually with the yellow type. The leaves are 3-7 cleft into narrow lobes and appear whorled around the stem.

CHECKER FIDDLENECK
Amsinckia tessellata

Borage Family
Boraginaceae

This plant is best admired with the eyes and not the hands. Also known as devil's lettuce, the white hairs on this plant can produce a very irritating rash if handled. Checker fiddleneck is an erect spring wildflower that grows 8-24 inches (20-60 cm) tall. It is common in dry sandy soils throughout most of the Mojave Desert. In the western Mojave, another species, *A. menziesii* var. *intermedia*, can occasionally be found.

GOLDEN FORGET-ME-NOT
Cryptantha confertiflora

Borage Family
Boraginaceae

Golden forget-me-not is a common perennial wildflower found in the mountains of southern Nevada and the east Mojave on dry, rocky limestone and in washes. The plant has several erect, bristly stems 6-17 inches (15-44 cm) tall from a stout, woody root. The flowers are yellow to cream-colored and $3^1/_2$-5 inches (9-13 mm) long.

YELLOW BUSH BEARDTONGUE

Keckiella antirrhinoides var. *microphylla*

Figwort Family
Scrophulariaceae

Bush beardtongue is found in rocky places mostly in piñon-juniper and Joshua tree woodlands of the southern and eastern Mojave to the Lake Mead region. It is a woody shrub 3-8 feet (1-2.5 m) high with branched, spreading stems and opposite leaves. The flowers are yellow and $1/2$-1 inch (15-23 mm) long with a widely expanded throat. The common name "beardtongue" alludes to the sterile fifth filament which, as this photo shows, is adorned with a beard of yellow hairs.

YELLOW MONKEYFLOWER
Mimulus guttatus

Figwort Family
Scrophulariaceae

Yellow monkeyflower is a common plant in wet places such as along streams and springs. It is a herbaceous perennial with hollow stems that grow 2-12 inches (5-30 cm) long. The leaves are opposite each other on the stem and oval in shape. The flowers are yellow, with hair and red dots in the throat. Since water is limited in the desert, this plant has a very localized distribution.

LESSER MOHAVEA
Mohavea breviflora

Figwort Family
Scrophulariaceae

Lesser mohavea is a common plant in the Death Valley region and is less common in the east Mojave around Kelso. It is a low growing spring wildflower 2-8 inches (5-20 cm) tall with glandular-hairy stems and leaves. The flowers are dark lemon-yellow with maroon spots in the throat. It is found in dry sandy and gravelly places from below sea level to 2500 feet (800 m) elevation in March and April.

INTERIOR GOLDENBUSH
Ericameria linearifolia

Sunflower Family
Asteraceae

This goldenbush is a showy perennial shrub 16-24 inches (40-60 cm) tall found on dry slopes and plains below 6500 feet (2000 m). It is a common member of Joshua tree and piñon-juniper woodlands (see p. 210). The plant blooms in spring and becomes densely covered with yellow daisies from March to May.

BLACK-BANDED RABBITBRUSH

Chrysothamnus paniculatus

Sunflower Family
Asteraceae

Black-banded, or Mojave rabbitbrush is a common fall flowering shrub found throughout the Mojave Desert in washes below 4000 feet (1200 m). The plant is a perennial rounded shrub with straight stems and fragrant foliage that grows 2-6 feet (60-200 cm) tall. The stems commonly have black bands about $^1/_2$ inch (12 mm) broad caused by a smut fungus.

SUNRAY
Enceliopsis argophylla

Sunflower Family
Asteraceae

Sunray is an impressive sunflower found in the Lake Mead region. The plant is 6-30 inches (15-80 cm) tall with flowers as much as 6 inches (15 cm) across on long, leafless stems. The silvery leaves are tufted at the base of the plant and felt-like to the touch. It is found mostly on eroded gypsum-bearing soils. In the Death Valley region are Panamint daisy (*E. covillei*) and naked-stemmed daisy (*E. nudicaulis*), which are uncommon sunrays found on stony hillsides and canyons.

GREEN ENCELIA
Encelia virginensis

Sunflower Family
Asteraceae

Green encelia is a perennial shrub 20-60 inches (50-150 cm) tall found on rocky slopes and plains of the east Mojave. Green encelia is one of four encelia species found in the California Desert. Its closest relative is Acton encelia (*E. actoni*), which is found in the southern Mojave and around Joshua Tree National Park. Brittlebush (*E. farinosa*) is another common relative generally found at lower elevations and is quite distinct with its branched flower arrangement. Rayless encelia (*E. frutescens*) is found below 2500 feet (800 m) in the eastern and southern Mojave.

MOJAVE COREOPSIS
Coreopsis calliopsidea

Sunflower Family
Asteraceae

Mojave coreopsis is a common spring wildflower found in the central and western Mojave. In the central Mojave north of Rainbow Basin it forms carpet displays in favorable years. Also in the Mojave Desert is Bigelow coreopsis (*C. bigelovii*). It occurs mostly in the southern and western Mojave, but extends to Death Valley. The spreading, leafy bracts at the base of the flower heads (outer phyllaries) are broad and rounded in Mojave coreopsis, while they are thin and narrow in Bigelow coreopsis.

CALIFORNIA TICKSEED
Coreopsis californica

Sunflower Family
Asteraceae

This tickseed is found on sandy plains, slopes, or washes at elevations below 4000 feet (1200 m). The leaves are located at the base of the plant and the stems are 2-12 inches (5-30 cm) tall. The yellow flowers are solitary on each stem and the flower head is $^1/_2$-$1^3/_8$ inches (10-35 mm) across. It is quite common in the southern Mojave Desert where it can create colorful displays.

DESERT SUNFLOWER

Geraea canescens

Sunflower Family
Asteraceae

Desert sunflower is a common spring wildflower sometimes found forming fields of color in sandy soils. The plant is erect and either single-stemmed or openly branched growing 8-30 inches (20-80 cm) tall. The flowers are golden yellow and fragrant. In favorable years desert sunflower forms magnificent displays in several locations including the lower fans of Death Valley, around Afton Canyon, and Pinto Basin in Joshua Tree National Park. In the Death Valley region, this plant is known locally as "desert gold."

DESERT MARIGOLD
Baileya multiradiata

Sunflower Family
Asteraceae

Desert marigold is a common spring wildflower found mostly on sandy plains and rocky slopes from the mountains of the eastern Mojave Desert to Nevada and Arizona. The plant grows 8-20 inches (20-50 cm) tall with several long straight stems, each with a single flower head. Desert marigold is very similar to woolly marigold (*B. pleniradiata*). The flower stems on desert marigold are leafless above the middle, and the flowers are larger with rays greater than $\frac{3}{16}$ inch (10 mm) long. Woolly marigold is not as common in the Mojave Desert.

LAX FLOWER
Baileya pauciradiata

Visitors to the sand dune regions of the Mojave Desert will find this common spring wildflower. Lax flower is a common plant that grows 8-24 inches (20-60 cm) tall. The stems are erect and covered with a loose, spreading wool. The flowers are light yellow with 4-8 small "petals" about $^1/_4$ inch (6 mm) long. As the flowers age, the rays, which are at first horizontal, turn papery and bend downward.

PAPERFLOWER
Psilostrophe cooperi

Sunflower Family
Asteraceae

Paperflower is a common desert shrub associated with Joshua tree woodlands and creosote bush scrub. The shrub has many ascending stems and grows 8-20 inches (20-50 cm) tall. The flowers are yellow and the rays become papery and paler with age. Paperflower is found on rocky desert mesas, plains, and hillsides mostly in the eastern and southern Mojave Desert. The plant blooms primarily in the spring, but will also bloom in the fall.

WOOLLY DAISY
Eriophyllum wallacei

Sunflower Family
Asteraceae

Woolly daisy is a low growing and tufted spring wildflower found in sandy soils. The plant has woolly stems and leaves, and is about 4 inches (10 cm) across. It occurs throughout the Mojave Desert in most habitats except high in the desert mountains. Around Barstow is the rare Barstow woolly daisy (*E. mohavense*), differing from this species by lacking ray flowers.

YELLOW-FROCKS
Eriophyllum ambiguum var. *paleaceum*

Sunflower Family
Asteraceae

Yellow-frocks is a small spring wildflower found in washes and on gravelly slopes in the northern and western Mojave Desert. It is a few- to many-branched plant 2-10 inches (5-25 cm) tall. The flowers are yellow and bloom April to June. Yellow-frocks is similar to woolly daisy (previous page), but is more erect instead of tufted.

GOLDFIELDS
Lasthenia californica

Sunflower Family
Asteraceae

Goldfields is a common spring wildflower found on sandy plains in the southern and western Mojave Desert. The plant grows erect, and while usually less than 5 inches (2 cm) tall, it can grow much taller in favorable years. As the common name implies, this wildflower can form vast yellow fields, sometimes with other desert wildflowers such as California poppy. It is very common in the Antelope Valley.

DESERT VELVET
Psathyrotes ramosissima

Sunflower Family
Asteraceae

Desert velvet is a compact, rounded shrub with velvet-woolly leaves. The plant is 2-5 inches (5-12 cm) tall and 2-12 inches (5-30 cm) broad. Also known as turtleback and velvet rosette, desert velvet grows in sandy soils at elevations below 3700 feet (1100 m). It is common in the Death Valley and Lake Mead regions, and at other relatively low elevations in the Mojave Desert. Also in the Mojave Desert is fan-leaf (*P. annua*) with greener leaves, and stems that are often purplish.

PYGMY CEDAR
Peucephyllum schottii

Sunflower Family
Asteraceae

Pygmy cedar is a common shrub in most of the Mojave Desert below 3000 feet (900 m) elevation on rocky slopes and in washes. It is a bushy, aromatic shrub that usually grows less than 5 feet (1.5 m) tall, though sometimes taller, with bright green leaves. Pygmy cedar is also known as desert-fir because of its narrow, almost fir-like leaves. The plant is quite common in the Death Valley region.

THURBER DYSSODIA
Thymophylla pentachaeta var. *belenidium*

Sunflower Family
Asteraceae

Thurber dyssodia is a low growing spring wildflower found mostly on limestone soils of the east Mojave Desert. The plant is strongly scented and grows 4-8 inches (10-20 cm) tall. The flowers are yellow and generally abundant on the plant. Thurber dyssodia grows in washes and rocky disturbed places between 3000-5000 feet (900-1500 m) elevation.

COOPER DYSSODIA
Adenophyllum cooperi

Sunflower Family
Asteraceae

Cooper dyssodia is a common perennial wildflower found from Death Valley to the eastern and southern Mojave. The plant is a low subshrub 12-20 inches (30-50 cm) tall with fragrant foliage. The flowers are yellow to orange-red. It grows in dry, sandy, open places, frequently along disturbed roadsides.

ANGELITA DAISY

Hymenoxys acaulis var. *arizonica*

Sunflower Family
Asteraceae

Angelita daisy is an uncommon perennial wildflower found in the mountains of the east Mojave (Clark, Providence, New York, and Spring). The plant is found between 4000-6500 feet (1200-2000 m) elevation, mostly in Joshua tree and piñon-juniper woodlands on rocky limestone slopes, but also on sandy flats. It grows 3-8 inches (8-20 cm) tall from a low branched crown. The hairy leaves are generally tufted at the base of the plant. The bright yellow flower heads are at the top of long unbranched stems.

COOPER GOLDFLOWER
Hymenoxys cooperi

Sunflower Family
Asteraceae

Cooper goldflower is found in Joshua Tree National Park and the higher mountains of the eastern Mojave. The plant is a biennial or short lived perennial, with a single stem usually branched above the middle into several flower heads. The alternate leaves are divided into narrow lobes. It grows in Joshua tree and piñon-juniper woodlands on dry slopes and flats between 4000-6600 feet (1200-2000 m). In the east and northern Mojave can also be found Nevada golden-eye (*Heliomeris multiflora*), a perennial with narrow stems, and narrow opposite leaves.

LOBED GROUNDSEL
Senecio multilobatus

Sunflower Family
Asteraceae

Lobed groundsel is found in the mountains of the east Mojave. The plant grows at elevations between 4000-6500 feet (1200-2000 m), frequently on dry slopes and limestone in Joshua tree and piñon-juniper woodlands. The erect stems are 6-18 inches (15-50 cm) tall with lobed leaves mostly on the lower half. This plant and Cooper goldflower (previous page) sometimes grow together. The leaves of the goldflower are divided into narrow segments, while the groundsel's leaves are broadly lobed.

SCALE BUD

Anisocoma acaulis

Scale bud is commonly found in washes and other sandy places in the Mojave and Colorado Deserts above 2000 feet (600 m) elevation. The flower heads are produced on leafless stems arising from a rosette of hairy, toothed leaves. The flowers are light yellow and bloom in spring from April to June, opening only during the day and closing at night. The leaves and flower stems bleed milky sap when cut.

SNAKE'S HEAD
Malacothrix coulteri

Snake's head is an erect spring wildflower occasionally found in washes and other sandy places below an elevation of 3500 feet (1000 m). The flowers are mostly pale yellow, though sometimes white. The plant is simple or few-branched and grows 4-20 inches (10-50 cm) tall. The lower leaves are mostly lobed, while the stem leaves are lobed or ear-like at the base.

DESERT DANDELION
Malacothrix glabrata

Desert dandelion is a common spring wildflower found on sandy plains, in washes, and at the base of shrubs. The flowers are light yellow with a red spot in the center when young. The plant is a low herb that grows 4-16 inches (10-40 cm) tall. The leaves are divided into narrow lobes and attached mostly at the base of the plant. This plant can form broad displays in the southern Mojave around Joshua Tree National Park. Also in the southern, western and northern Mojave is yellow-saucers (*M. sonchoides*), with broad, usually toothed or widely-lobed leaves.

YELLOW TACK-STEM
Calycoseris parryi

Sunflower Family
Asteraceae

Yellow tack-stem is a common spring wildflower in sandy soils below 6000 feet (1800 m) elevation. The plant grows 4-12 inches (10-30 cm) high and has dark tack-shaped glands on stems that exude milky sap when cut. The leaves are 1-4½ inches (3-12 cm) long and those lower are divided into narrow lobes. This plant is a yellow flowered relative of white tack-stem (p. 46).

KEYSIA
Glyptopleura marginata

Keysia is a tufted ephemeral found throughout the Mojave Desert on sandy flats mostly between 2000-4500 feet (600-1300 m). It is common in the central and western Mojave. The sweetly scented flowers open late in the morning and vary from white to creamy-yellow. The leaves are lobed with a conspicuous white margin.

Orange and Red Flowers

California Poppy
Antelope Valley

STREAM ORCHID, HELLEBORINE
Epipactis gigantea

Orchid Family
Orchidaceae

Stream orchid is only occasionally found in the Mojave Desert, mostly because its habitat is uncommon in desert regions. It occurs on perennial seeps and springs in scattered locations. The plant grows 1-2 feet (30-60 cm) tall from a creeping rootstock. The flowers are traditionally shaped for an orchid and brownish to reddish colored.

DESERT MARIPOSA LILY
Calochortus kennedyi

Desert mariposa lily is found mostly in the western and eastern Mojave Desert in creosote bush scrub and piñon-juniper woodlands. The flower color is variable from mostly red in the western Mojave, orange in the eastern Mojave, and yellow in the mountains of the eastern Mojave (variety *C. k.* var. *munzii* in the Panamint, Clark, and Providence Mountains). The plant is erect or twisted, 4-8 inches (10-20 cm) tall, producing 1-6 flowers on a single stem. While this plant resembles California poppy, its three-petaled flowers are characteristic.

CALIFORNIA POPPY
Eschscholzia californica

Poppy Family
Papaveraceae

California poppy is California's state flower. It is capable of forming broad displays in the western Mojave's Antelope Valley (see p. 112). The flowers are orange with petals about 1-2 inches (25-50 mm) long. In favorable years the Antelope Valley becomes a wildflower showcase with California poppy the main attraction. A good place to see good displays is around the Antelope Valley California Poppy Reserve near Lancaster. Notice that the flowers have four petals.

SCARLET FOUR-O'CLOCK
Mirabilis coccinea

Four-O'Clock Family
Nyctaginaceae

Scarlet four-o'clock is an occasional wildflower found in the mountains of the east Mojave. The plant has one to several erect stems and grows 1-2 feet (30-60 cm) tall on dry rocky slopes, along washes, and on plains in Joshua tree and piñon-juniper woodlands. The deep-red flowers open at night and are about ½ inch (12-15 mm) long.

WILD RHUBARB
Rumex hymenosepalus

Buckwheat Family
Polygonaceae

Wild rhubarb is a common herbaceous perennial that grows each year from a cluster of tuber-like roots. The plant is common in the Mojave Desert in sandy, usually disturbed places such as washes and roadsides. The pinkish flowers are in a compact cluster and turn into reddish winged fruits that give the plant most of its color. Wild rhubarb grows 2-4 feet (60-120 cm) tall with wavy-margined leaves and reddish stems.

DESERT MALLOW
Sphaeralcea ambigua

Desert mallow is a popular perennial shrub found mostly on dry rocky slopes and occasionally in washes. The petals are red-orange to apricot in color. The shrub is very showy in spring and grows 20-40 inches (50-100 cm) tall. The leaves are covered with star-shaped hairs that can be quite irritating. The rare Panamint desert mallow (*S. rusbyi* var. *eremicola*) is a similar plant with deeply divided, nearly compound leaves. It occurs from the Death Valley region to the Clark Mountains in the east Mojave.

ARIZONA FIRECRACKER
Ipomopsis arizonica

Phlox Family
Polemoniaceae

Arizona firecracker is an erect spring wildflower found in washes and rocky places. It grows in the mountains of the eastern Mojave above 4500 feet (1400 m) with piñon-juniper woodlands. The plant is 4-12 inches (10-30 cm) tall with red, tubular flowers that flare at the ends. As can be guessed, the plant is popular with hummingbirds.

DESERT INDIAN PAINTBRUSH

Castilleja angustifolia

Figwort Family
Scrophulariaceae

Indian paintbrush is a very characteristic wildflower found in most of the Mojave Desert with sagebrush scrub, and in piñon-juniper and Joshua tree woodlands. The plant is frequently found growing up through other plants, using them for support. Most of the color in the bright red spike comes from 3-5 lobed bracts around each yellow-green flower. The species has a very broad range, extending to western Canada, Wyoming, and New Mexico.

WOOLLY INDIAN PAINTBRUSH
Castilleja foliolosa

Figwort Family
Scrophulariaceae

Woolly Indian paintbrush just enters the Mojave Desert along the western border and is fairly common in the hills west of the Antelope Valley. The plant is a low, bushy perennial less than 20 inches (50 cm) tall with white-woolly leaves and stems. Most of the bright color is from the conspicuous bracts and calyces which mostly conceal the greenish flowers. This Indian paintbrush is found in dry, open and rocky places below 5000 feet (1500 m) elevation.

EATON FIRECRACKER
Penstemon eatonii

Figwort Family
Scrophulariaceae

Eaton firecracker is a common spring perennial growing mostly in the mountains. It is found on gravelly slopes and in sandy washes. It associates mostly with piñon-juniper woodlands, but is also found in sagebrush and creosote bush scrubs. The long, tubuler flowers are scarlet to deep red and clustered in leaf axils on stems 1-3 feet (30-100 cm) tall. Eaton firecracker is very popular with hummingbirds.

UTAH FIRECRACKER
Penstemon utahensis

Utah firecracker is a many-stemmed perennial wildflower found occasionally in the east Mojave mountains of California and Nevada (Kingston, New York, and Spring Mountains). The flowers are red to carmine and arranged along vertical flower stalks 1-2 feet (30-60 cm) tall. The plant occurs in rocky soils, usually on gentle slopes, with sagebrush or in piñon-juniper woodlands.

Pink to Lavender Flowers

Owl's Clover in a Field of California Poppy
Antelope Valley

WEAKSTEM MARIPOSA LILY
Calochortus flexuosus

Lily Family
Liliaceae

Weakstem mariposa lily is a straggling spring wildflower found from the Lake Mead region to the eastern Mojave Desert on dry-stony slopes. The plant is weak-stemmed and either sprawling on the ground or intertwined through other plants. The flowers are lilac with a purple spot and yellow band on each petal. There are 1-2 basal leaves that soon wither after the plant starts flowering.

WILD HYACINTH, BLUE DICKS
Dichelostemma capitatum

Lily Family
Liliaceae

Wild hyacinth is a common perennial wildflower from underground corms. The leafless stems are 1-2 feet (30-60 cm) long and topped with a cluster of 2-15 flowers. There usually are two to three narrow leaves 6-16 inches (15-40 cm) long and $^1/_4$-$^1/_2$ inch (5-12 mm) wide at the bast of the stems. The bell-shaped flowers are violet to pink-purple. It is found throughout the Mojave Desert in dry, open places, usually supported by other shrubs.

DESERT WINDFLOWER
Anemone tuberosa

Buttercup Family
Ranunculaceae

Desert windflower is an attractive perennial herb found in the mountains of the east Mojave. The plant grows from a tuberous root and the mostly single stem is 4-12 inches (10-30 cm) tall. The flowers are whitish to rose color and about $^1/_2$ inch (10-14 mm) long. It grows on rocky, limestone slopes and ledges, usually from cracks in the rocks.

STICKY-RINGSTEM
Anulocaulis annulatus

Four-O'Clock Family
Nyctaginaceae

Ringstem is a perennial herbaceous wildflower found at lower elevations of the Mojave Desert including the Death Valley and Lake Mead regions. The stems grow erect and have a characteristic brown ring on the internode between the leaves. The flowers are pale pink and about $^1/_3$ inch (8 mm) long. The leaf nodes are wide-spaced and the leaves are rounded with stiff hairs, each hair with an enlarged gland at the base. It grows in dry, sandy washes and on rocky slopes.

GIANT FOUR-O'CLOCK
Mirabilis multiflora

Four-O'Clock Family
Nyctaginaceae

Giant four-o'clock is a common herbaceous perennial from a thick tuberous root. The plant is mostly a prostrate shrub with stems 12-32 inches (30-80 cm) long and thick leaves. The exceptionally showy flowers are rose-purplish to magenta and $1^1/_2$ inches (35-45 mm) long. It grows on desert plains and in sandy washes mostly in Joshua tree and piñon-juniper woodlands or lower elevation plant communities. It is especially common in the mountains of the east Mojave and on Cima Dome.

HAIRY SAND VERBENA

Abronia villosa

Four-O'Clock Family
· Nyctaginaceae

Sand verbena is a common member of the sand dune community and is especially common in the Devil's Playground/Kelso Dunes area of the east Mojave, and on the dunes around Stove Pipe Wells in Death Valley. The plant has trailing stems 4-20 inches (10-50 cm) long with thick, rounded leaves. The showy, tubular flowers are pink to magenta. In the east and west Mojave is also the Mojave sand verbena (p. 10), which has white to pink flowers and seeds with two wings instead of five.

WINDMILLS
Allionia incarnata

Four-O'Clock Family
Nyctaginaceae

Windmills is a common spreading annual or short-lived perennial. The stems are sticky, trail close to the ground, and grow to about 30 inches (75 cm) long. The flowers are rose-magenta. What looks like a single flower is actually a head of three separate flowers. Windmills is also known as trailing four o'clock and can be found on dry stony slopes and plains, mostly in creosote bush scrub.

DESERT FIVE-SPOT
Eremalche rotundifolia

Mallow Family
Malvaceae

Desert five-spot is a common spring wildflower found frequently at lower elevations (below 3800 feet, 1200 m) in washes, on bajadas, and other open places. The rose-pink to lilac flowers open mid-morning and have a dark purple blotch at the base of each petal. It grows 4-16 inches (10-40 cm) tall. The leaves are round and usually purplish-red. The common name comes from the dark blotches found on each petal.

PRINCE'S ROCK-CRESS
Arabis pulchra

Mustard Family
Brassicaceae

Prince's rock-cress is a perennial herb found in the mountains of the Mojave Desert on canyon slopes, desert plains, and in washes. The plant is usually single-stemmed and 8-24 inches (20-60 cm) tall. The flowers are rose colored and produce a long, narrow fruit $1^1/_2$-$2^3/_4$ inches (4-7 cm) long that is either pendent or spreading. Rock-cress is frequently found growing up through other shrubs.

ROCK LIVE-FOREVER
Dudleya saxosa ssp. *aloides*

Stonecrop Family
Crassulaceae

Rock live-forever is a common leaf succulent found in the desert mountains of the eastern and southern Mojave Desert up to 5500 feet (1700 m) elevation. It is very common in Joshua Tree National Park and in the mountains of the Mojave National Preserve growing in dry rocky places. In the Panamint Mountains near Death Valley is the rare subspecies, *D. s.* ssp. *saxosa*, with smaller leaves and red-tinged petals. Another related plant found in the east Mojave is Arizona live-forever (*D. pulverulenta* ssp. *arizonica*) with flat, wide leaves.

MOJAVE REDBUD
Cercis occidentalis var. *orbiculata*

Legume Family
Fabaceae

Mojave redbud is an unusual find in the Mojave Desert. It can be found in the Spring Mountains of southern Nevada, including Red Rock Canyon National Conservation Area near Las Vegas. The plant is a large shrub or small tree to 15 feet (4.5 m) tall with winter deciduous leaves. The magenta-pink flowers are prolific in spring usually before the leaves appear and are followed by reddish seed pods.

ARIZONA LUPINE
Lupinus arizonicus

Legume Family
Fabaceae

Arizona lupine is one of many lupines found in the Mojave Desert. It is quite common in Death Valley and Joshua Tree National Parks, and around Lake Mead. The plant has dark pink to magenta flowers and grows 4-20 inches (10-50 cm) tall in sandy washes and open places mostly below 2000 feet (900 m). In good years Arizona lupine is capable of broad displays. Also in the Mojave Desert is Coulter's lupine (*L. sparsiflorus*, p. 172) which is very similar, but has blue flowers and narrower leaflets.

WIDE-BANNERED LUPINE
Lupinus microcarpus

Legume Family
Fabaceae

Wide-bannered lupine is a common spring wildflower found in the western and central Mojave. It is variable in flower shape and color, but one characteristic that separates this from other lupine species is the whorled arrangement of the flowers. The flowers are generally pink to purple, but can also range between white and yellow. It is found in grasslands and other dry, open areas mostly below 5000 feet (1500 m) elevation.

ELEGANT LUPINE
Lupinus concinnus

Legume Family
Fabaceae

Elegant lupine is a very common lupine growing in most regions of the Mojave Desert. The leaves are densely covered with hairs and the stems are usually reddish. The flowers are pink to purple, with a white or yellowish spot on the banner. It is very similar to desert lupine (*L. shockleyi*) which is hairless on top of the leaves and has deep blue to purplish flowers. Both plants occur in sandy soils, and while they can grow 12 inches (30 cm) tall, they are usually much smaller.

NEWBERRY MILKVETCH
Astragalus newberryi

Legume Family
Fabaceae

Newberry milkvetch is a very attractive wildflower found from the eastern Mojave to Death Valley. The plant is a low, tufted perennial with pink-purple flowers that bloom April to June. The seed pods are inflated and densely covered with white hairs. It grows in gravelly and rocky places mostly above 4000 feet (1200 m) elevation with sagebrush and in piñon-juniper woodlands.

PRAIRIE CLOVER
Dalea searlsiae

Legume Family
Fabaceae

Prairie clover is an uncommon herbaceous perennial found in the mountains of the east Mojave and southern Nevada. It is usually associated with sagebrush and piñon-juniper woodlands. The rose to purple flowers are arranged in a terminal elongated spike on stems 12-20 inches (30-50 cm) long. The plant is a favorite browse of local cattle.

BLUE FLAX
Linum lewisii

Flax Family
Linaceae

Blue flax is a perennial spring wildflower distributed from the Mississippi River to the Pacific Coast. The plant is 6-30 inches (15-75 cm) tall, with slender, erect stems and narrow leaves. In the Mojave Desert the flowers are mostly lavender to near white, instead of blue. Blue flax is most commonly found in the east Mojave on dry slopes and ridges. Seldom encountered in the east Mojave is a related flax with yellow flowers (*L. puberulum*). It grows 4-12 inches (10-30 cm) tall in the New York and Clark Mountains.

WHITE RHATANY
Krameria grayi

Rhatany Family
Krameriaceae

White rhatany is a shrub found in the central, eastern, and southern Mojave Desert in rocky or sandy places below 4000 feet (1200 m). The plant is a thorny, densely-branched shrub growing 12-28 inches (30-70 cm) high. The flowers are purple with reflexed sepals that resemble petals. Pima rhatany (*K. erecta*) is a relative found mostly in the central and southern Mojave Desert. The petal-like sepals of pima rhatany are cupped and pink.

PINK PHLOX
Phlox stansburyi

Phlox Family
Polemoniaceae

Pink phlox is an especially attractive wildflower found in the mountains of the east Mojave of California and Nevada mostly in Joshua tree and piñon-juniper woodlands. The plant is a woody-based, openly branched perennial that grows 2-8 inches (5-20 cm) tall. It is sometimes found stretching up through other shrubs. The pink to white flowers are very showy and can densely cover the plant.

BROAD-FLOWERED GILIA

Gilia cana ssp. *speciformis*

Phlox Family
Polemoniaceae

Broad-flowered gilia is found in the eastern Mojave Desert on mostly volcanic or basaltic sands. The plant is erect, 4-12 inches (10-30 cm) tall, with densely cobwebby leaves located mostly at the base of the stems. The flowers are tubular with pink lobes and a throat that is bluish in the upper half and yellow in the lower half. Several other species of *Gilia* are also found in the Mojave Desert and are very difficult to tell apart.

BROAD-LEAVED GILIA
Gilia latifolia

Phlox Family
Polemoniaceae

Broad-leaved gilia is a common spring wildflower found on rocky slopes, bajadas, and in desert washes. The leaves are round, almost holly-like, and located at the base of the plant. The flowers are dark pink and either grow within the leaves or on erect stems 4-12 inches (10-30 cm) tall. Broad-leaved gilia is found in the Mojave Desert at elevations below 2000 feet (600 m) in usually very hot, exposed environments.

BRISTLY GILIA
Langloisia setosissima ssp. *setosissima*

Phlox Family
Polemoniaceae

Bristly gilia is related to lilac sunbonnets on the next page. It can either be a tufted spring wildflower 1-3 inches (2-7 cm) high, or prostrate with stems 4 inches (10 cm) long. The flowers are light to deep violet, sometimes with darker streaks. The floral tube is more than twice the length of the lobes. It grows in sandy to gravelly places such as in washes and on plains and bajadas.

LILAC SUNBONNETS
Langloisia setosissima ssp. *punctata*

Phlox Family
Polemoniaceae

Lilac sunbonnets is a spring wildflower found in desert washes and on gravelly or rocky slopes and plains. The flowers are white to light blue, with various amounts of purple spots and two yellow dots on each petal. The plant is a tufted or simple-stemmed wildflower growing 1-6 inches (3-15 cm) tall with toothed leaves. Sunbonnets differs from bristly gilia by having flower lobes almost as long as the flower tube below. The lobes of bristly gilia are shorter, usually only $^1/_3$ the length of the tube.

DESERT CALICO
Loeseliastrum matthewsii

Phlox Family
Polemoniaceae

Desert calico is a tufted spring wildflower that grows 1-6 inches (3-15 cm) tall throughout the Mojave Desert in washes and other sandy places. The plant has several horizontal branches and toothed leaves. The flowers are strongly bilateral, white to deep rose-purple in color, and $^1/_2$-$^3/_4$ inch (11-21 mm) long. The petals have bright maroon arches at their base and square to notched tips. It is very similar to Schott gilia (*L. schottii*), which has shorter petals with pointed tips and flowers that are weakly to moderately bilateral.

PURPLE MAT
Nama demissum

Waterleaf Family
Hydrophyllaceae

Purple mat is a common spring wildflower found on sandy washes and plains. The narrow stems are 1-8 inches (3-20 cm) long and the plant grows low to the ground. The flowers are blue-purple to pink. The leaves are narrow, $1/_2$-$1^1/_2$ inches (1-4 cm) long, and taper toward the stem. In the Death Valley region is another variety, *N. d.* var. *covillei*, with spoon- to diamond-shaped leaves.

PALMER PHACELIA
Phacelia palmeri

Waterleaf Family
Hydrophyllaceae

Palmer phacelia is a locally distributed plant found on the gypsum-bearing mud hills around Las Vegas and Lake Mead. The plant grows very erect to a height of about 2 feet (60 cm) and resembles a Christmas tree. The flowers are lavender to light blue and clustered into several scorpion tail-like inflorescences off the side of the main stem. The plant is very ill-smelling if handled. Palmer phacelia is a biennial requiring two years to mature and bloom.

DEATH VALLEY PHACELIA
Phacelia vallis-mortae

Waterleaf Family
Hydrophyllaceae

Death Valley phacelia is a common spring wildflower found in sandy soils usually using other shrubs for support. The stems are 8-24 inches (20-60 cm) long. The flowers vary from white to lavender and violet. The plant is found mostly from Death Valley through the east Mojave to Lake Mead. It is very similar to the blue flowered wild heliotrope (*P. distans*) and can be very difficult to distingush. In general, the flowers of wild heliotrope are blue, and the leaf lobes tend to be more rounded.

CALTHA-LEAVED PHACELIA
Phacelia calthifolia

Waterleaf Family
Hydrophyllaceae

Caltha-leaved phacelia is found from the Death Valley region of California and western Nevada southward to Barstow. The plant is an erect spring wildflower, 4-12 inches (10-30 cm) tall, and found in sandy, soils below 3000 feet (1000 m). The leaves are round with sticky hairs. The purple to violet flowers are funnel- to bell-shaped and $^1/_4$-$^1/_2$ inch (8-12 mm) long.

NOTCH-LEAVED PHACELIA
Phacelia crenulata

Waterleaf Family
Hydrophyllaceae

Notch-leaved phacelia is a very common spring wildflower found on sandy washes and slopes throughout the Mojave Desert. This ill-scented plant is usually single stemmed, though sometimes branched, and grows 3-16 inches (7-40 cm) tall. The flowers are deep violet to blue-purple and $^1/_4$-$^1/_2$ inch (6-10 mm) long. The stems and leaves are short-hairy, glandular, and known to produce a skin rash similar to poison oak in some people.

FREMONT PHACELIA
Phacelia fremontii

Waterleaf Family
Hydrophyllaceae

Fremont phacelia is a common spring wildflower found in sandy or gravelly soils throughout most of the Mojave Desert. The plant is 3-12 inches (7-30 cm) tall with erect to spreading stems. The leaves are located mostly near the base of the plant and are deeply divided. The funnel- to bell-shaped flowers are $^1/_4$-$^1/_2$ inch (7-15 mm) long and blue to lavender, with a yellow throat. Occasionally this wildflower forms small, mass displays.

GOODDING VERBENA
Verbena gooddingii

Goodding verbena is associated with piñon-juniper and Joshua tree woodlands and found in washes and on rocky slopes. It is quite common in the mountains of the east Mojave and the Spring Mountains of Nevada at elevations between 4000-6500 feet (1200-2000 m). The plant is a low growing perennial with stems 8-18 inches (20-45 cm) long. The flowers are purplish in color and about $\frac{1}{2}$ inch (12 mm) long.

THISTLE SAGE
Salvia carduacea

Thistle sage is a common spring wildflower found in sandy or gravelly soils of the western and central Mojave Desert. The plant grows erect 4-20 inches (10-50 cm) tall and is covered with a dense, white wool on the stems, leaves, and flower heads. The fragrant leaves are located at the base of the plant and are dissected with wavy margins and short spines. The flowers are lavender, rarely blue or white, with fringed margins and exerted brick-red anthers.

MOJAVE SAGE
Salvia mohavensis

Mint Family
Lamiaceae

Mojave sage is a locally common plant found in scattered locations of the Mojave Desert. The shrub usually grows less than 3 feet (1 m) tall with green, wrinkled leaves. The blue to lavender flowers are a little over $^1/_2$ inch (15-16 mm) long and clustered at branch ends. It grows in dry rocky washes and canyons below 5000 feet (1500 m) from the Little San Bernardino Mountains northward to the Clark Mountains and eastward to Lake Mead (Newberry Mountains).

CHIA

Salvia columbariae

Mint Family
Lamiaceae

Chia is a common spring wildflower found below 4000 feet (1200 m) in washes and other disturbed places. The leaves are found mostly at the base of the plant, and when crushed, emit an odor similar to skunk. The flowers are lavender to deep blue and arranged in one to three tight globular heads around the stems. The seeds are very nutritious and were valued by Native Americans. The plant grows 4-20 inches (10-50 cm) tall with one to several stems.

MOJAVE OWL'S-CLOVER
Castilleja exserta ssp. *venusta*

Figwort Family
Scrophulariaceae

Owl's-clover is commonly associated with the poppy fields in the western Mojave Desert (see p. 124). The plant is exceptionally showy with deep velvet-pink bracts and yellow-tipped flowers. The plant grows with erect, slender stems 4-16 inches (10-40 cm) tall. In the Antelope Valley, carpets of this plant can be mixed with California poppy, or the plant can form solo displays.

SCENTED BEARDTONGUE
Penstemon palmeri

Figwort Family
Scrophulariaceae

Scented beardtongue is a common spring wildflower found mostly on limestone soils and can be prolific in sandy washes. The flower stalks grow as high as 6 feet (1.8 m). The very fragrant flowers are pink to rose with darker guidelines in the inflated throat. The plant is found at elevations between 4000-6000 feet (1200-1800 m) in the mounains of Death Valley and the eastern Mojave. It is associated mostly with Joshua tree woodlands and piñon-juniper woodlands.

BIGELOW MONKEYFLOWER
Mimulus bigelovii

Figwort Family
Scrophulariaceae

Bigelow monkeyflower is a common wildflower found mostly in washes but also on rocky hillsides. The plant is a densely-hairy annual usually 2-5 inches (5-13 cm) tall but in favorable years grows to 10 inches (25 cm). The flowers are rose to dark magenta, and the throat is golden yellow on the bottom. In favorable years this monkeyflower can form relatively dense displays.

DEATH VALLEY MONKEYFLOWER
Mimulus rupicola

Figwort Family
Scrophulariaceae

Death Valley monkeyflower is an attractive spring wildflower growing in the mountains bordering Death Valley. The flowers are pinkish, sometimes faintly so, with a magenta-purple spot on each lobe. The leaves are tufted and 1-3 inches (2-7 cm) long. It is a rare plant that can be found in shaded limestone crevices on steep canyon walls.

DESERT WILLOW
Chilopsis linearis

Bignonia Family
Bignoniaceae

Desert willow is an exceptional desert tree restricted to desert washes below an elevation of 5000 feet (1500 m). The tree is winter deciduous and grows about 15 feet (4.5 m) tall. The flowers are pink to almost white, with purplish lines in the throat. The tree begins to leaf out in late spring and can bloom from late spring through summer into fall. Desert willow is not really a willow and the common name is derived from the willow-like leaves. Desert willow is a desirable landscape tree.

HOLE-IN-THE-SAND PLANT
Nicolletia occidentalis

Sunflower Family
Asteraceae

Hole-in-the-sand plant is found in the western and southern Mojave Desert in sandy soils. This unpleasantly-scented perennial grows between 4-8 inches (10-20 cm) tall in a small depression in the sand from a deep taproot. The ray flowers are mostly pink, and the disk flowers are yellow, aging pink.

MOJAVE ASTER

Xylorhiza tortifolia

Sunflower Family
Asteraceae

Mojave aster, also known as desert aster, is a common plant found on desert plains and rocky slopes. The shrubs are bushy and grow 8-26 inches (20-60 cm) tall. The flowers are very ornamental, light blue to white, with a yellow center. It is very common in Joshua tree woodlands at elevations mostly between 3000-5500 feet (900-1700 m). It is quite common in Joshua Tree National Park and around the mountains of the east Mojave.

TIDY FLEABANE
Erigeron concinnus

Sunflower Family
Asteraceae

Tidy fleabane is a small perennial wildflower 4-12 inches (10-30 cm) tall, with a thickened and branched root crown. The flowers have rays that are white, pink or blue, with a yellow disk. The plant grows in sandy to rocky soils on slopes and plains with creosote bush or in piñon-juniper and Joshua tree woodlands. It can be occasional to common from the mountains and valleys of the east Mojave to the mountains around Death Valley.

PINK PEREZIA
Acourtia wrightii

Sunflower Family
Asteraceae

Pink perezia is an occasional shrub found in the Mojave desert of Arizona and Utah on desert plains. The plant is an attractive perennial herb growing 16-24 inches (40-60 cm) tall. The flowers grow in clusters and cover the plant with color in spring. Pink perezia just enters the Mojave desert from other areas in Utah and Arizona and can be found in Washington County, Utah, and in Mojave County, Arizona around Dolan Springs.

Blue and Purple Flowers

Indigo Bush
Lake Mead National Recreation Area

DESERT LARKSPUR
Delphinium parishii

Buttercup Family
Ranunculaceae

Desert larkspur is a common spring wildflower found below 7500 feet (2300 m) elevation on gravelly plains and in washes. In the southern Mojave around Joshua Tree National Park the flowers are dark blue to purplish, while in the eastern and northern Mojave the flowers are a sky- blue color (shown). The plant grows 7-36 inches (17-90 cm) tall and is nearly leafless, with most of the leaves at the base of the plant.

DESERT CANDLE
Caulanthus inflatus

Mustard Family
Brassicaceae

Desert candle is a common plant found in the central and western Mojave Desert. This unusual plant grows 8-28 inches (20-70 cm) tall between 2000-5000 feet (600-1500 m) elevation. The simple stems are erect and conspicuously inflated. In the mountains of the eastern Mojave is a similar plant, thick-stem wild cabbage (*C. crassicaulis*). The upper leaves of desert candle are clasping around the stem, while the leaves of wild cabbage are not. The stems of wild cabbage are also less inflated and purplish.

MINIATURE LUPINE
Lupinus bicolor

Legume Family
Fabaceae

Miniature lupine is an annual wildflower very common in grasslands with California poppy and occasionally found along the desert's edge in Joshua tree woodlands. It is frequently found in the Antelope Valley extending east to Joshua Tree National Park. The plant is usually less than 10 inches (25 cm) tall.

COULTER'S LUPINE
Lupinus sparsiflorus

Legume Family
Fabaceae

In the Mojave Desert, Coulter's lupine is found mostly in the east Mojave. It is very similar to Arizona lupine (p. 136), but has blue flowers and the leaflets are narrower. It can be locally common on gravelly and sandy flats or in washes. The plant is a slender-stemmed ephemeral usually less than 1 foot (30 cm) tall, but in favorable years can grow taller. This lupine is capable of producing small, local displays.

ROYAL MOJAVE LUPINE
Lupinus odoratus

Legume Family
Fabaceae

Royal Mojave lupine is a common spring wildflower with light green leaves, found in sandy or gravelly soils of the western and central Mojave Desert. The plant is 6-12 inches (15-30 cm) tall, though the flower stems can extend horizontal from the center. The violet-scented flowers are blue-purple with a white or yellow spot on the banner petal. In favorable years, royal lupine forms colorful displays. In the east Mojave occurs yellow-eyes (*L. flavoculatus*). Yellow-eyes is shorter than 6 inches (15 cm) tall, with flowers less than $^1/_3$ inch (8 mm) long.

LAYNE MILKVETCH
Astragalus layneae

Legume Family
Fabaceae

Layne milkvetch is a common spring wildflower and the most widespread dapple-pod in the Mojave Desert. The flowers are whitish, with purple on the tips of the petals. The plant is perennial, blooming in the spring, with stems less than 6 inches (16 cm) long. The reddish fruit has wavy hairs and has a characteristic sickle-shaped with no inflation. Layne milkvetch is found on sandy plains and washes and in disturbed soils below 5000 feet (1550 m) elevation.

FREMONT DAPPLE-POD
Astragalus lentiginosus var. *fremontii*

Legume Family
Fabaceae

Fremont dapple-pod is a densely hairy dapple-pod found in open sandy places of the east Mojave. The stems are either erect or reclining and 4-20 inches (10-50 cm) long. The flowers are purple and are followed by an inflated, papery pod. Other varieties of *A. lentiginosus* occuring in the Mojave Desert include the shining milkvetch (var. *micans*) from the Eureka Dunes, the rare Sodaville milkvetch (var. *sesquimetralis*) from northern Death Valley, var. *albifolius* from the western Mojave, and var. *variabilis* from the southern Mojave.

NUTTALL MILKVETCH

Astragalus nuttallianus var. *imperfectus*

Legume Family
Fabaceae

Nuttall milkvetch is a slender, prostrate wildflower found mostly in the eastern Mojave, but also extends to the central Mojave and Death Valley. It grows in sandy or stony places below 5200 feet (1600 m). The flowers are about $\frac{1}{4}$ inch (4-7 mm) long and whitish, tinged lilac, or as shown, purplish.

MOJAVE INDIGO BUSH

Psorothamnus arborescens

Legume Family

Fabaceae

This plant is one of three related members of the genus *Psorothamnus* found in or near the Mojave Desert. All three are about 3-4 feet (1-1.3 m) tall with spine-tipped branches. They are found on desert plains, slopes, or washes. This species shown is found in most of the Mojave Desert except in the eastern half. The second common indigo bush, *P. fremontii*, is found in the central and eastern Mojave (see p. 168). The third species, *P. polydenius*, is found in the central Mojave around Barstow.

PURPLE CYMOPTERUS
Cymopterus multinervatus

Purple cymopterus is an occasional perennial wildflower found on dry slopes and plains mostly in the eastern Mojave, but also found along the north slope of the San Bernardino Mountains. The plant grows in Joshua tree and piñon-juniper woodlands at elevations between 3500-6000 feet (1000-1800 m).

DESERT CANTERBURY BELLS
Phacelia campanularia ssp. *vasiformis*

Waterleaf Family
Hydrophyllaceae

Canterbury bells is a common spring wildflower found mostly in the southern Mojave, but extends into the eastern Mojave as far north as the Providence Mountains. The plant is 7-22 inches (18-55 cm) tall, with deep blue funnel-shaped flowers 1-1¹/₂ inches (25-40 cm) long. It grows in dry, sandy or rocky places. This plant is known to cause a skin dermatitis similar to poison oak on some people.

LACY PHACELIA
Phacelia tanacetifolia

Waterleaf Family
Hydrophyllaceae

Lacy phacelia is a common spring wildflower found in the southern and central Mojave Desert northward to the Panamint Mountains on sandy to gravelly slopes and plains. The plant is stiffly-erect, few-branched, and 6-40 inches (15-100 cm) tall. The blue flowers are about $^1/_4$ inch (6-9 mm) wide and tightly congested into densely hairy heads that uncoil like a scorpion tail. The stamens are also very long and exserted past the petals.

PAPER-BAG BUSH
Salazaria mexicana

Mint Family
Lamiaceae

Paper-bag bush is a common shrub of the Mojave Desert found in dry washes and canyons below 5000 feet (1500 m). The plant grows into a rounded shrub 1$^1/_2$-3 feet (0.5-1 m) tall, with rigid and almost spine-like branches. The flowers are white to light violet on the upper lip, and the lower three-lobed lip is violet to purple. The calyx produces an inflated, papery bag that turns pinkish or reddish.

CARNOSA or BLUE SAGE
Salvia dorrii var. *pilosa*

Mint Family
Lamiaceae

Carnosa sage is a very common sage found on desert plains and washes in piñon-juniper and Joshua tree woodlands. The plant is a low shrub 16-24 inches (40-60 cm) tall, with white-scaly leaves and stems. The flowers are blue to purple and subtended by blue or purple hairy bracts. Carnosa sage is highly variable with respect to flower color and leaf shape and size. In the northern Mojave Desert is the variety *S. dorrii* var. *dorrii*, with scaly or hairless flower bracts.

DEATH VALLEY SAGE
Salvia funerea

Also known as funeral sage, this spiny-leaved shrub is endemic to dry washes and limestone canyon walls in the Death Valley region. The plant is white-woolly and densely leafy. It grows about 2 feet (60 cm) tall or can drape 3 feet (1 m) down canyon walls. The flowers are violet or blue and partially embedded in white wool. The leaves are almost holly-like and pleasantly fragrant when crushed.

THOMPSON BEARDTONGUE
Penstemon thompsoniae

Figwort Family
Scrophulariaceae

Thompson beardtongue is a rare plant in California found only in the eastern Mojave's Clark Mountains. It is slightly more common in the mountains of southern Nevada and northwest Arizona. The plant is a low, gray mat forming tuft 1-2 inches (2-5 cm) tall and 4-10 inches (10-25 cm) across. The tublular flowers are blue-violet and $^1/_2$-$^3/_4$ inch (13-18 mm) long.

DESERT HOARY ASTER
Machaeranthera canescens

Sunflower Family
Asteraceae

Hoary aster is an occasional aster found on the Kelso Dunes and is also found in Joshua tree woodlands at elevations between 3300-6600 feet (1000-2000 m) in the east Mojave, in southern Nevada, and occasionally elsewhere. The flower heads have blue-purple rays, with a yellow center. The plant is 12-20 inches (10-50 cm) tall with spreading or erect stems, and mostly an annual or short-lived perennial. The flowers bloom from spring into summer and occasionally in the fall.

Cactus Flowers

Teddy-Bear Cholla Gardens
Joshua Tree National Park

PENCIL CHOLLA

Opuntia ramosissima

Pencil cholla is very characteristic with its narrow joints that are seldom more than $^3/_8$ inch (10 mm) thick and long radiating spines. The plant grows 1-5 feet (30-150 cm) tall and can either be an erect shrub or a low-growing mat. The flowers are greenish when they first open, but turn reddish or salmon color as they age. Pencil cholla grows on dry slopes, plains, and in washes throughout the Mojave Desert below 4000 feet (1200 m).

BUCKHORN CHOLLA
Opuntia acanthocarpa

Cactus Family
Cactaceae

Buckhorn cholla is a common cactus in the Mojave Desert, mostly at middle elevations below 4200 feet (1300 m). The plant grows tree-like or shrubby 3-6 feet (1-2 m) tall on sandy plains or rocky slopes. The flowers are yellow-orange to orange-red, with reddish anther filaments, and the fruit is dry and spiny. The bumps on the stem, called tubercles, are generally three times longer than wide.

GOLDEN or SILVER CHOLLA
Opuntia echinocarpa

Which common name to use depends on the color of the spines. The flowers are greenish-yellow, with pale-green anther filaments, and the fruit is dry and spiny. The plant grows throughout most of the Mojave Desert below 4600 feet (1400 m) on dry plains and occasionally in washes. The plant is an intricately-branched shrub 2-4 feet (60-120 cm) tall, with a short, woody trunk and a dense crown. The bumps on the stems, called tubercles, are about twice as long as wide.

WHIPPLE CHOLLA
Opuntia whipplei

Cactus Family
Cactaceae

Whipple cholla is not found naturally in California, but is found in the Nevada and Arizona sections of the east Mojave Desert. It is usually bushy or mat-forming, 1-2 feet (30-60 cm) tall, but can also be erect and shrubby to 6 feet (2 m). The flowers are yellow or greenish-yellow and about 1 inch (3 cm) wide. The yellow fruits of whipple cholla are spineless and fleshy at maturity, unlike those of silver cholla, which are spiny and dry at maturity.

BEAVERTAIL CACTUS
Opuntia basilaris

Cactus Family
Cactaceae

Beavertail cactus lacks the characteristic spines that are typical of the cactus family. The plant is well protected though, and the brownish dots on the pads should be avoided since they contain very small spines called glochids that are very irritating and difficult to remove. Beavertail grows only about 1 foot (30 cm) tall with several spreading stems on desert plains and slopes. The flowers are a brilliant magenta and are very popular with desert wildflower enthusiasts.

ENGELMANN PRICKLY-PEAR

Opuntia engelmannii

Cactus Family
Cactaceae

This prickly-pear is a sprawling plant usually less than 2 feet (60 cm) high, with oval pads greater than 6 inches (15 cm) wide. It grows mostly in piñon-juniper and Joshua tree woodlands, but occasionally can be found at lower elevations. The flower petals are all yellow. A similar prickly-pear, *O. phaeacantha*, has pads less than 6 inches (15 cm) wide and yellow flowers with red at the base of the petals. Botanically, these two cacti are closely related and have been a classification problem.

PANCAKE PRICKLY-PEAR
Opuntia chlorotica

Pancake prickly-pear is an erect, almost tree-like cactus with a stout trunk. The pads are nearly round and have many reflexed, yellow spines. The flowers are yellow, sometimes tinged red at the base, and bloom late in spring. The plant grows 3-8 feet (1-2.5 m) tall in mostly piñon-juniper and Joshua tree woodlands at elevations between 3000-5000 feet (900-1500 m). It is especially common in and around the mountains of the east Mojave.

MOJAVE PRICKLY-PEAR
Opuntia erinacea

Cactus Family
Cactaceae

Mojave prickly-pear is a common clumping cactus that usually grows less than 12 inches (30 cm) tall, but can grow as high as 20 inches (50 cm). The flowers are yellow and age to a reddish color. The plant grows on sandy plains or rocky slopes with creosote bush or in piñon-juniper woodlands. The spine density and length is variable and plants with dense, flexible, threadlike spines and larger flowers have been called grizzly bear or old man cactus.

PYGMY BARREL CACTUS
Sclerocactus johnsonii

Pygmy barrel is an uncommon cactus found mostly on rocky slopes and washes from Death Valley, through Nevada (Lake Mead region) into Arizona. The plant has 4-8 central spines that are straight or curved, but not hooked. The flowers are usually pink or magenta, but plants around Searchlight, Nevada commonly have yellow flowers. The plant grows 4-10 inches (10-25 cm) tall and 2-4 inches (5-10 cm) in diameter. In the central Mojave around Barstow is Mojave fish-hook cactus, *S. polyancistrus*, with 9-11 central, sometimes hooked spines.

HEDGEHOG CACTUS
Echinocereus engelmannii

Cactus Family
Cactaceae

Hedgehog cactus is a common cactus found throughout the Mojave Desert on gravelly fans and plains, and on rocky slopes. The plant usually has 5-15 (or more) heads in a clump less than 3 feet (1 m) across. The flowers are purplish-magenta to lavender. The spines are variable in size and color and can either be dark reddish-brown to yellowish, pinkish, or gray.

CLARET CUP CACTUS
Echinocereus triglochidiatus

Cactus Family
Cactaceae

Claret cup, or Mojave mound cactus, is an especially spectacular mound cactus found mostly in piñon-juniper and Joshua tree woodlands at elevations above 3500 feet (1000 m). The plant forms a dense clump with up to several hundred heads 16 inches (40 cm) tall. In spring the top of the plant becomes covered with bright scarlet flowers. Some of the best shows of this plant are in the east Mojave around Cime Dome and Lanfair Valley.

BARREL CACTUS, BISNAGA
Ferocactus cylindraceus

Cactus Family
Cactaceae

The barrel cactus is a common columnar cactus found throughout the Mojave Desert on gravelly plains and rocky slopes. The plant is usually single trunked, less than 6 feet (1.8 m) tall, and 12-16 inches (30-40 cm) thick with reddish or yellowish spines. The flowers are borne at the top of the plant in a ring and have yellow petals. This plant has been exploited by illegal over-collecting.

DESERT FOXTAIL CACTUS

Cactus Family

Escobaria vivipara var. *deserti*

Cactaceae

Desert foxtail cactus is found mostly in the mountains of the east Mojave on stony limestone slopes and washes. The plant is usually single stemmed, $2^3/_4$-6 inches (7-15 cm) tall, and $2^3/_4$-$3^1/_2$ inches (7-9 cm) in diameter. The flower petals are 1 inch (2-3 cm) long and yellowish, yellow-green, or tinged pink. The plant is found in Joshua tree woodlands and can be especially common in the Clark and Ivanpah Mountains.

MOJAVE FOXTAIL CACTUS

Escobaria vivipara var. *rosea*

Cactus Family
Cactaceae

Mojave foxtail cactus is a rare cactus found from the New York Mountains in the east Mojave northward into southern Nevada. The plant is $2^3/_4$-7 inches (7-18 cm) tall, and unlike corkseed cactus, the central spines are not hooked. The flowers are magenta to purplish and 1-2 inches (3-5 cm) in diameter. This plant is threatened by illegal collection.

CORKSEED CACTUS
Mammillaria tetrancistra

Cactus Family
Cactaceae

Corkseed cactus is one of the more desirable cactus finds in the Mojave Desert. The plant is 2-10 inches (5-25 cm) tall, mostly with single stems. There are usually 1-4 central spines, of which one or more will be hooked, and more than 25 white, radial spines. The pinkish flowers are $1-1\frac{1}{2}$ inches (25-40 mm) wide. The plant is uncommon on sandy or rocky slopes and plains in scattered locations throughout the Mojave Desert.

Name Changes

Mojave Desert Wildflowers	Other Botanical Name
Adenophyllum cooperi	Dyssodia cooperi
Amsonia tomentosa	Amsonia brevifolia
Anulocaulis annulatus	Boerhavia annulata
Castilleja angustifolia	Castilleja chromosa
Castilleja exserta var. venusta	Orthocarpus purpurascens var. ornatus
Chaetopappa ericoides	Leucelene ericoides
Chamaesyce albomarginata	Euphorbia albomarginata
Dalea searlsiae	Petalostemon searlsiae
Datura wrightii	Datura meteloides
Dichelostemma capitatum	Dichelostemma pulchella
Dudleya pulverulenta ssp. arizonica	Dudleya arizonica
Ericameria linearifolia	Haplopappus linearifolius
Escobaria vivipara	Coryphantha vivipara
Ferocactus cylindraceus	Ferocactus acanthodes
Ipomopsis arizonica	Ipomopsis aggregata ssp. arizonica
Heliomeris multiflora	Viguiera multiflora
Krameria erecta	Krameria parvifolia
Langloisia setosissima ssp. punctata	Langloisia punctata
Lasthenia californica	Lasthenia chrysostoma
Lesquerella tenella	Lesquerella palmeri
Loeseliastrum matthewsii	Langloisia matthewsii
Loeseliastrum schottii	Langloisia schottii
Lotus strigosus	Lotus tomentellus
Mirabilis multiflora	Mirabilis froebelii
Mirabilis coccinea	Oxybaphus coccineus
Nolina parryi	Nolina wolfii
Oenothera californica ssp. avita	Oenothera avita
Opuntia engelmannii	Opuntia phaeacantha
Phlox stansburyi	Phlox viridis ssp. compacta
Psorothamnus arborescens	Dalea fremontii
Purshia mexicana var. stansburyana	Cowania mexicana var. stansburiana
Purshia tridentata var. glandulosa	Purshia glandulosa
Sclerocactus johnsonii	Neolloydia johnsonii
Sclerocactus polyancistrus	Echinocactus polyancistrus
Senna armata	Cassia armata
Thymophylla pentachaeta	Dyssodia pentachaeta
Xylorhiza tortifolia	Machaeranthera tortifolia

Index